ANIMATION

ANIMATION

How to Draw Your Own Flipbooks,
and Other Fun Ways to Make Cartoons Move

Patrick Jenkins

▲

Addison-Wesley Publishing Company, Inc.

Reading, Massachusetts ■ Menlo Park, California ■ New York

Don Mills, Ontario ■ Wokingham, England ■ Amsterdam ■ Bonn

Sydney ■ Singapore ■ Tokyo ■ Madrid ■ San Juan

Paris ■ Seoul ■ Milan ■ Mexico City ■ Taipei

Library of Congress Cataloging-in-Publication Data

Jenkins, Patrick.
    Animation : how to draw your own flipbooks, and other fun
ways to make cartoons move / by Patrick Jenkins.
        p.   cm.
    Summary: Includes instructions for creating drawings that give
the illusion of various kinds of movement and special effects. Also
describes several early motion picture devices.
    ISBN 0-201-56757-1
    1. Animated films – Technique – Juvenile literature.
[1. Animation (Cinematography)   2. Drawing – Technique.]
I. Title.
NC1765.J46   1991
741.5'8 – dc20   91-26233
                                       CIP
                                       AC

Originally published in Canada as *Flipbook Animation* by
Kids Can Press, Ltd., of Toronto.

Edited by Laurie Wark
Interior design by N. R. Jackson
Set in 10 point Optima Medium by
Compeer Typographic Services Limited

1 2 3 4 5 6 7 8 9-AL-9594939291
First printing, September 1991

Addison-Wesley books are available at special discounts for bulk
purchases by schools, institutions, and other organizations. For
more information, please contact:

Special Markets Department
Addison-Wesley Publishing Company
Reading, MA 01867
(617) 944-3700 x2431

Text stock contains over 50% recycled paper

CONTENTS

Acknowledgements

I would like to thank the following people and organizations for their assistance in the production of this book:

The Creative Artists In Schools program of the Ontario Arts Council and the Inner City Angels of Toronto who gave me the opportunity to work with hundreds of children in schools throughout Ontario; the Office of Research Administration at York University who gave me a research grant to explore animation and publish my own flipbooks; the Toronto Animated Image Society for their generous support of my work and the art of animation; the people at Kids Can Press, especially Valerie Hussey, Ricky Englander, Laurie Wark and Nancy Jackson, who encouraged and guided me through the various stages of producing this book.

To my parents Ivan and Jean Jenkins
and to Pamela Williams.
Thank you for all your help and encouragement
over the years.

Introduction to flipbooks

When you watch an animated cartoon, what you are really seeing is a series of pictures one after the other. Take a look at the strip of movie film shown on this page. Look closely and you'll notice that each drawing of the fish is slightly different from the previous drawing. When these pictures, or frames, are flashed quickly in front of your eyes, the fish appears to swim into view. In an animated movie, you see 24 pictures every second! That means that during an average 90-minute movie, you watch about 130 000 pictures.

You can make your own movie in a flipbook, but don't worry, you won't have to draw 130 000 pictures. A flipbook is simply a small pad of paper with a drawing on each page. Just like the frames of a filmstrip, each drawing in a flipbook is slightly different from the drawing on the preceding page. When you flip the pages (like those shown below), you have the impression that you are watching a short animated movie.

Flipbooks are fun and easy to make, but you'll need to know the five flipbook basics on the next few pages before you begin making your own.

1. The pad

Make your flipbooks on small notepads or memopads (like the ones you use to write telephone messages on). Pads that are about 8 × 13 cm (3 × 5 inches) in size work well. The pads should have at least 50 pages, but pads with 96 pages are ideal. It's best if the paper in the pad is plain white. These pads are available at stationery and office supply stores.

You can recycle some paper to make your own pads by binding small piles of paper together with an elastic, binder clip or staple. If you do this, be sure to get all the paper evenly aligned along the open edge.

For the projects in this book, always work from the back of the pad (the page next to the cardboard backing) to the front of the pad. You will put the pages down on top of each other. This will allow you to see through the pages to what you have already drawn. So, when you are ready to flip the pad, you will flip from the back to the front.

It is best to keep your images on the half of the pad that is closest to the open edge. This is the most visible part of the pad. If you draw your pictures too close to the binding of the pad, you will find it difficult to see them when you flip your flipbook.

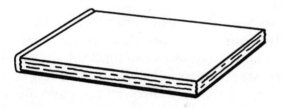

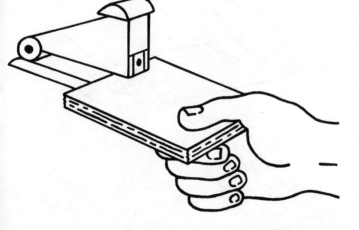

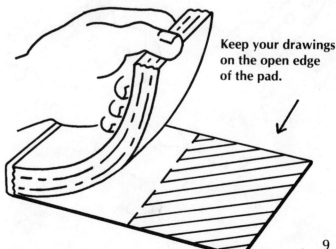

Keep your drawings on the open edge of the pad.

2. Drawing a character

Usually when you draw a picture, you add as much detail to it as you like because you are only drawing it once. But in a flipbook, you will be drawing your pictures many times over. If the character is too complicated to draw, you will find that it takes a lot of time and energy to keep drawing it. So it is important to keep your drawings very simple. Try to use as few lines as possible and use simple shapes, such as circles, squares and triangles, when you draw your characters.

Look at the drawings below. Notice how few lines have been used to draw them. These characters will be easy to draw over and over again.

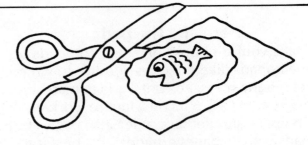

3. Stencils

Throughout this book you will use a stencil for each of your flipbook projects. A stencil is a page with a drawing of your character on it that you will trace over and over again in creating your flipbook. It is important to use the stencil when you are learning to animate so that you keep your character the same shape and size as you draw it over and over again.

Go over the lines of your stencil drawing with a pen or marker. Since you will be placing the pages of the flipbook on top of your stencil to trace it, you will have to be able to see your stencil through the page. Be sure to hold the stencil in place as you put a page over it, so that it doesn't move.

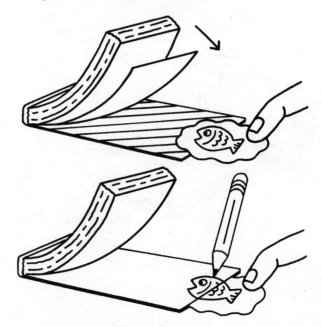

4. Moving your character

The secret to smooth animation is to move your character just a tiny bit between pages. Move your stencil about the width of a toothpick (about 2 mm) each time to produce smooth animated movement. If you move your character a large distance between pages, you will find that the animated movement is too fast and rough. Do your flipbook animation in pencil first. That way if you make a mistake, it will be easy to fix. When you have finished your animation, you can go over the outlines of your characters with a fine black marker. This will make your animation easier to see.

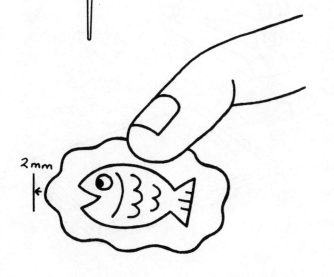

Move your stencil about the width of a toothpick— that's only about 2 mm, or 1/13 inch!

2mm

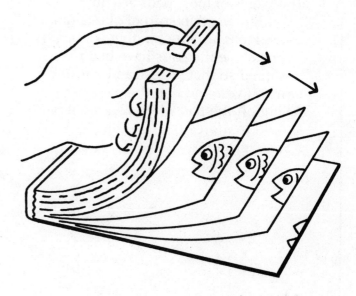

5. Flip the pages and watch your movie!

If it seems to be taking a while to see your results, reward yourself by flipping the pages and looking at your movie. You should check your movie every now and then anyway to make sure the animation is working. Usually you'll need to do at least ten drawings before you will have movement in your animation. Your movie will become more and more interesting as you add more pages.

Several projects in this book can be seen in flipbook form at the edges of this book. Flip the corner of this book as you go along to see if you are getting the proper effect in your flipbook. It's best to make the flipbooks in the order that they appear in this book, since most of them build on techniques learned in previous projects.

Reinforcing the binding of your flipbook

The pages of most pads are held together by a thin strip of glue along one edge. This glue binding is not very strong since the pads have been designed so that pages can be torn off easily. If you find that the pages are falling off the pad when you flip it, you should reinforce the binding. Here are a few suggestions:

1. Wrap an elastic band around the pad next to the binding.

2. Put a binder clip around the binding.

3. Use a heavy-duty stapler to staple the pages together next to the binding.

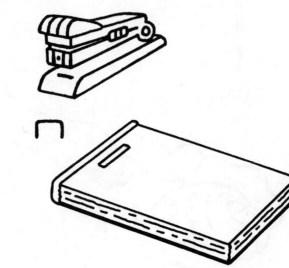

The two-page flip

You can animate a character using just two pictures in the "two-page flip."

You'll need
a pencil
a piece of paper about 8 cm × 13 cm
(3 × 5 inches)

1. Fold the piece of paper in half as shown.

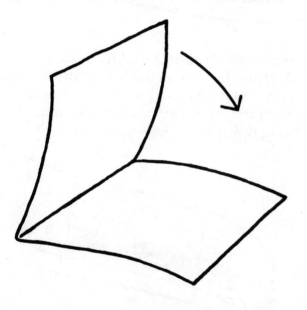

2. On the inside page, draw a stick figure with its arms and legs down and a puzzled look on its face. Press hard with your pencil so that you can see the figure through the outside page when it's folded over.

3. On the outside page trace the head and body of the stick figure, but this time draw the arms and legs going up and a happy look on its face.

4. Use your pencil to curl the outer page as shown, and roll the pencil and page back and forth very quickly. The figure will jump for joy.

1. LET'S MOVE

Let's start moving our characters. Begin by making the first flipbook project, "Make a fish swim," to discover the basics of making a character move. Then go on to the next two projects, "Loop the loop" and "Hot pursuit," where you'll expand your undersea adventure by making the fish do some fancy swimming as it tries to avoid a hungry whale. Do these three projects in order using the same pad and you'll end up with a short animated movie. Then try the next projects "Flap your wings" and "A cloud floats by." In these flipbooks you'll make a bird look like it's really flying high up in the sky. In the final two projects "Out for a walk" and "Creating a background," you can animate a character walking down the street. Have fun!

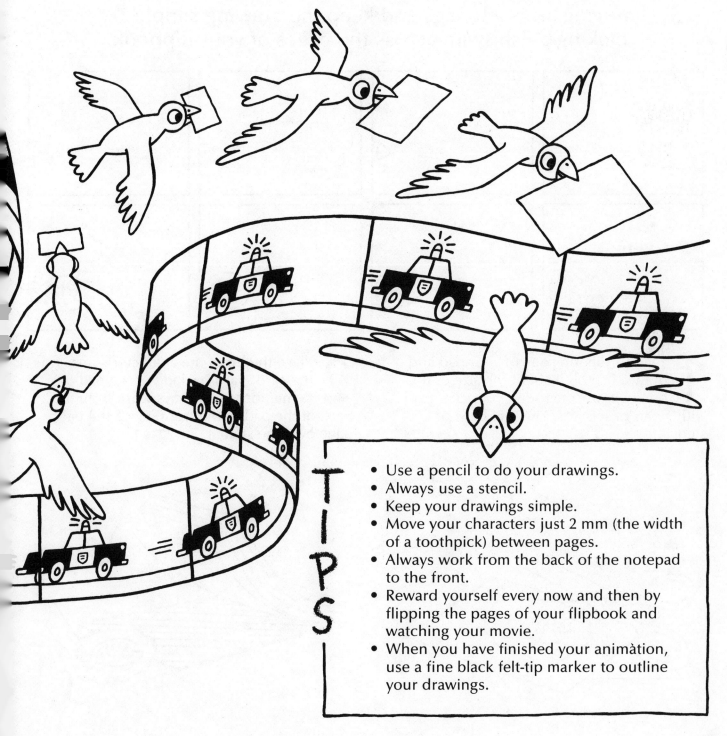

TIPS

- Use a pencil to do your drawings.
- Always use a stencil.
- Keep your drawings simple.
- Move your characters just 2 mm (the width of a toothpick) between pages.
- Always work from the back of the notepad to the front.
- Reward yourself every now and then by flipping the pages of your flipbook and watching your movie.
- When you have finished your animàtion, use a fine black felt-tip marker to outline your drawings.

MAKE A FISH SWIM

For your first character, choose one that doesn't have moving arms and legs and keep the drawing simple. Try making a fish swim across the pages of your flipbook.

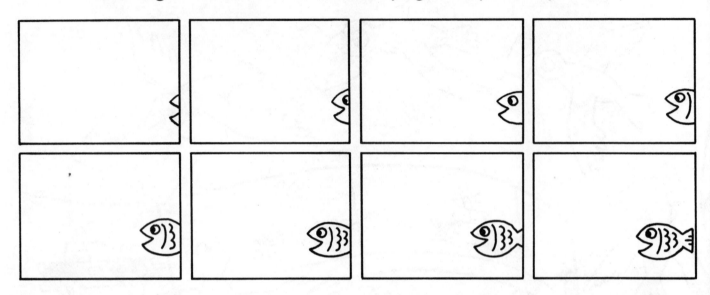

1 Tear off the top page of your pad and draw a fish on it about the size of the one below. Cut around your character with a pair of scissors. This will be your stencil.

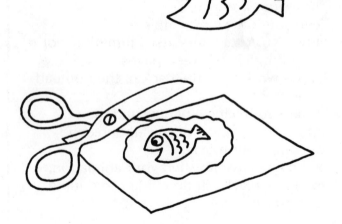

2 Place the tip of the character's nose on the cardboard backing of the pad. Remember you always work from the back of the pad to the front. Place the back page over the stencil.

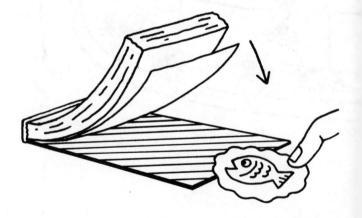

3 You should be able to see the stencil through the page. Trace what you can see.

4 Take the stencil out and place it directly on top of your last drawing. Then push the stencil in about 2 mm (about the width of a toothpick). Put the next page down and trace what you can see.

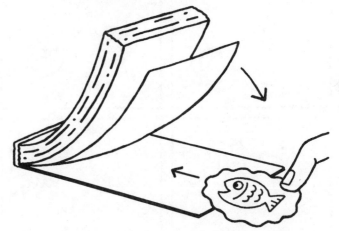

5 Repeat this process on each page so that your character is moving in just a little farther each time. Keep animating your character until all of it can be seen on the page.

6 Flip the edge of your pad to see if the character is moving. In this example, a fish will swim onto the page. If you flip the pad from front to back, the fish will swim backwards.

You've probably got lots of pages left on your pad, so turn to the next activity and we'll make the fish do some tricks.

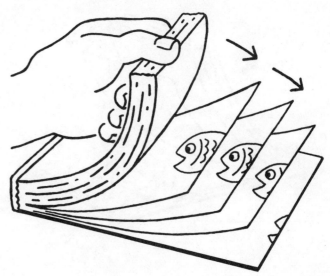

LOOP-THE-LOOP

Now that your fish is swimming, you can make it do a loop-the-loop. Use the same pad and fish stencil that you used on the last flipbook (pages 16–17).

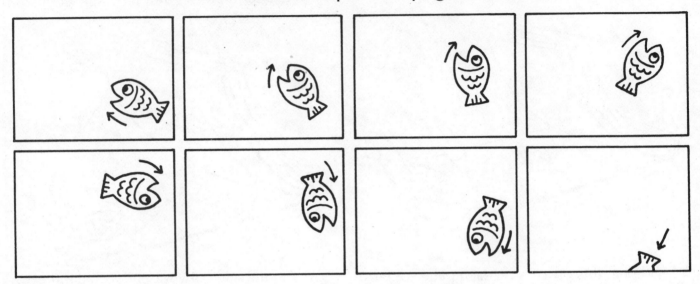

1 Place your stencil over your last drawing of the swimming fish. Now push the stencil in 2 mm, then twist the stencil up, so that the nose of your fish turns up about 2 mm. Put the next page down.

2 Trace the stencil with your pencil.

3 Repeat this process on each page, pushing and turning your stencil a tiny bit each time.

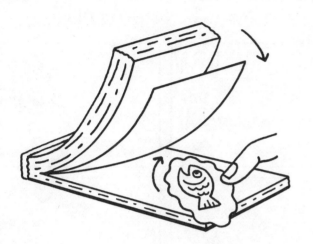

TIP

Keep your fish on the half of the pad that is closest to the open edge (where you flip the pages). If you find that your fish is swimming too far into the pad or off the page, give your fish less push and more twist on each move.

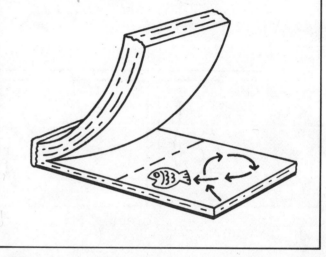

4 Flip the pages. Now your fish should swim onto the page and swim in a circle. After your fish has done its loop-the-loop, keep animating it until it swims off the bottom edge of your pad. When your fish's tail disappears off the bottom of the page, you can stop drawing.

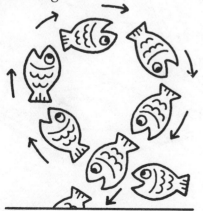

5 Flip the pages and watch your fish swim onto the page and do a loop-the-loop. You can add another character to your underwater adventure. Turn the page to find out how.

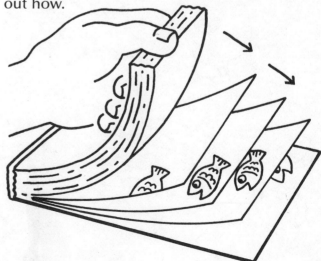

HOT PURSUIT!

Add some excitement to your underwater scene by having a second character chase your fish. Choose something bigger than your fish, such as a whale, shark or octopus. Use the same pad you used on the previous two projects.

1 Tear another page off the front of your notepad. Draw a whale or other big fish on this page and cut around it to make your new stencil. This new, bigger character will chase your fish.

2 Flip the pages of your pad and stop at a page when your fish is halfway through the loop where its nose is pointing down. Put the tip of the nose of the whale on the top edge of the page.

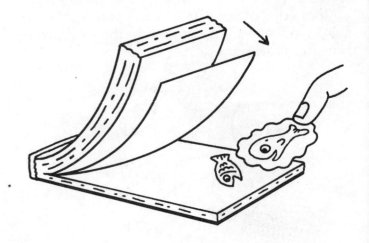

3 Place the next page over it. Trace what you can see of the whale stencil.

4 Place your whale stencil directly over top of the last whale drawing. Now push the stencil down 2 mm and twist it 2 mm towards the centre of the pad. Move your whale so that it follows the fish. Put the next page over top and trace what you can see of the whale stencil.

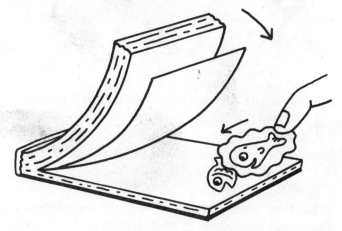

5 Repeat this procedure. When you flip the pages, your whale should chase your fish. Continue to move your whale until it has chased the fish off the page and its tail has disappeared.

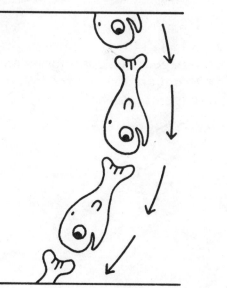

6 Now your flipbook is complete. When you flip the pages, you should have a short adventure movie just like the one in the top right-hand corner of this book.

FLAP YOUR WINGS

Animating a bird flying is a beautiful effect. You'll do this animation in two steps. First you'll use one stencil of the bird's body to make the bird move across the page. Then you'll go back and use a second set of stencils to add the wings.

1 Tear off the top page of your notepad. Draw the bird's beak, head, body and tail, but don't draw the wings. Draw a line where the wings will be attached to the bird's body as shown below. Now erase the part of the bird's body that is above this wing line. Then erase the part of the bird's body that is below the wing line. This will be your stencil.

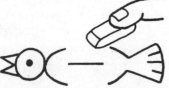

2 Cut out your stencil and place just the tip of the bird's beak on the cardboard backing of the pad. Place the next page over top and trace what you can see of the stencil.

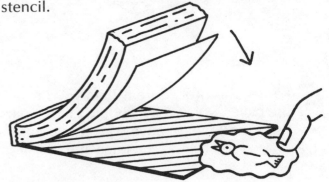

3 Place your stencil over the last drawing and push the stencil into the pad about 2 mm. Place the next page over top and trace what you can see with your pencil.

4 Repeat this procedure on each page, until all of the bird's body appears on the page. Then continue to animate the bird so that it gradually turns up and flies off the top edge of the pad.

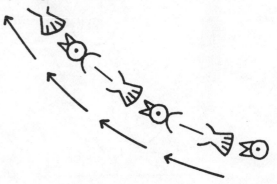

5 Now let's add some wings. Tear off another page from the front of your notepad and trace the 6 wing positions shown below onto your new stencil page. Be sure to include the number that is under each wing position on your stencil, since we'll be using these wing positions in consecutive order.

#1 #2 #3 #4 #5 #6

6 Flip the pages of your flipbook and let the bird fly onto the page. Stop flipping at the page where the first wing line is visible on the bird's body. Place the wing position number 1 under this page so that the bottom of the wing lines up with the wing line. Trace this wing position onto the bird's body with your pencil. Trace the wing position number very lightly, too, so that you will know what wing position you traced here.

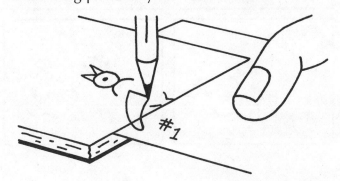

7 Go to the next page and line up wing number 2 so that the bottom of it lines up with the wing line. Trace this wing onto the bird's body. Trace the wing number very lightly. Repeat this procedure until you reach wing number 6. Now lower your bird's wings. To do this, go to your next page and trace wing number 6. Now work your way

down to number 1 until the wings have reached their lowest point. Then start to bring the wings up again (positions 1 to 6).

Go back and erase the wing position numbers. Then draw in the top and bottom of the bird's body around the wing. Turn the page to find out how to add more detail to your high-flying adventure.

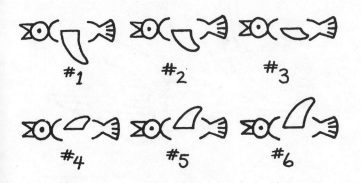

#1   #2   #3

#4   #5   #6

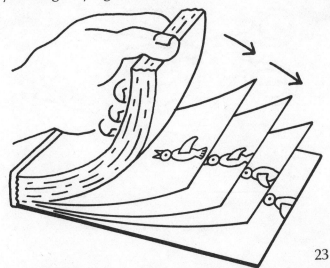

A CLOUD FLOATS BY

Now that your bird is flying, let's add a cloud to the background to make it look as if your bird is flying high in the sky.

1 Tear off a page from the front of the notepad you used for the bird flipbook. Draw a cloud on this page and cut around it for your stencil.

2 Since we want the cloud to float in the opposite direction to the bird, place your cloud in the middle of the cardboard backing of the pad.

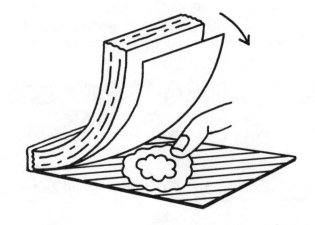

3 Put down the last page of the book and trace the entire cloud stencil.

4 Place the cloud stencil directly on top of the last drawing. Push your stencil 2 mm towards the open edge of the pad where the bird is flying. Put down the next page and trace what you can see of the cloud stencil. Repeat this procedure on each page of the pad.

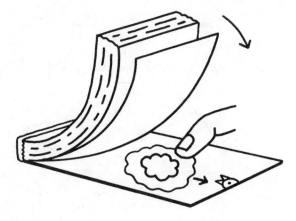

5 When the bird and the cloud overlap, the bird's body will block out the cloud. So don't trace the part of the cloud that shows through the bird's body. Repeat this procedure until the cloud floats off the open edge of the page.

6 When you flip the pages, the bird will appear to fly in and pass in front of the cloud. This gives the illusion that the bird is closer to us than the cloud.

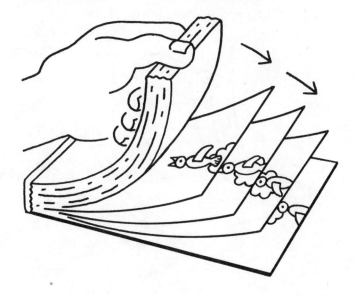

Out for a Walk!

Making characters walk is one of the biggest challenges in animation. Your figure must move forward and the position of the arms and legs must change as well. An easy way to animate walking is by using several stencils.

#1   #2   #3   #4   #5   #6

1 On the last page of the pad, draw a line near the bottom edge. This line will be the ground on which your character will walk. Repeat this procedure until you have traced the ground line on about 30 pages.

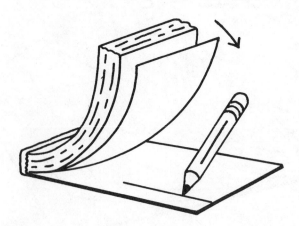

2 Tear six pages off the front of your note pad. Trace or copy one of the figures shown above on each page, including the number that is under each character. These six pages will be your stencils.

3 Using stencil 1, place the tip of the character on the cardboard backing of the pad. Put the back page of the pad over the stencil, making sure that your character's front foot is touching the ground line. Trace what you can see of the stencil. Lightly write in the number of the stencil so you can remember what stencil to use next.

4 Place stencil 2 directly on top of the last drawing. Push the stencil into the pad about 2 mm, making sure that your character's feet are still touching the ground. Place the next page on top of the stencil and trace what you can see, including the number of the stencil.

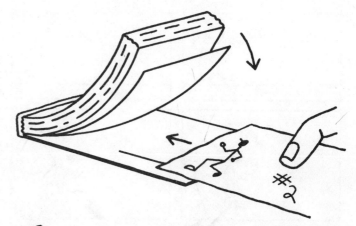

5 Repeat this procedure in order with stencils 3 to 6. When you have finished with stencil 6, return to stencil 1 and repeat the cycle.

Continue to move the character in until it disappears into the half of the pad that is closest to the glue binding.

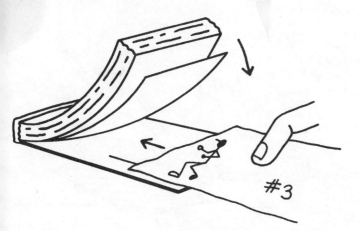

6 Flip the pages and watch your movie. It will look as if your character is walking on the ground line. If something doesn't look right, check the order of the stencils that you used. You may have used the stencils out of order. If it looks o.k., gently erase the stencil numbers from each page. Read on and we'll add some scenery to our walk.

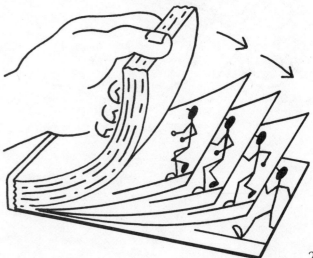

CREATING A BACKGROUND

Now that your character is walking, use the same notepad to give it an interesting place to walk. By using another stencil, you can create the illusion that the character is walking in a park.

1 Tear off a page from the front of your notepad. Draw a tall tree on this page for your stencil.

2 You'll move the tree in the opposite direction to the walking person just as you did with the bird and cloud on page 24. Place your tree in the middle of the cardboard. Make sure that the bottom of the tree is touching the ground line.

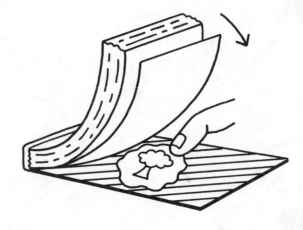

3 Put the last page of the book over the tree stencil and trace the entire tree.

4 Place your tree stencil directly on top of the last drawing. Push your stencil 2 mm towards the open edge of the pad where the person is walking. Put down the next page and trace what you can see of the tree stencil.

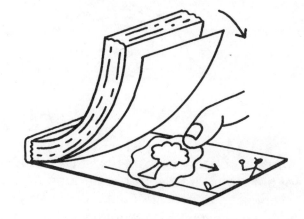

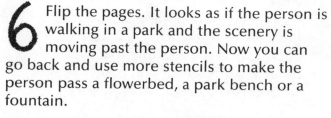

5 Repeat this procedure until the tree and the walking person meet each other. When the person and the tree overlap, the person's body will block out part of the tree. Repeat this procedure until the tree moves off the open edge of the page.

6 Flip the pages. It looks as if the person is walking in a park and the scenery is moving past the person. Now you can go back and use more stencils to make the person pass a flowerbed, a park bench or a fountain.

Cel animation

You've probably noticed that it takes a lot of time to re-draw your background on every page of your flipbook. Movie animators have invented a technique called cel animation to save themselves time and work.

In cel animation there are two elements: the background and the characters. The background is a painting that is usually done in watercolours on paper. The second part of cel animation is a piece of clear plastic called a cel. The moving characters are drawn on cels, similar to the way you've been drawing characters in your flipbooks. Then colour is added to the character by painting it with an opaque (not see-through) paint.

In flipbook animation, you use the corners of the pages as a method of keeping the drawings lined up. In cel animation, both the background and the cels have a set of holes punched into

them. These are called registration holes and they are placed in a series of pegs to keep everything lined up. When the image to be animated is ready to be shot with a camera, the cel is laid on top of the background. The character's painted body blocks out part of the background, but the rest of the background shows through the clear plastic around the character. The animation camera takes one or two pictures of the cel and background, then the first cel is taken away and a new cel is placed on the background and photographed. The advantage to this system is that the background has to be drawn only once.

If the animators want to show the characters moving past some moving scenery, then the background is painted on a long piece of paper. This long drawing is then moved a little bit at a time in the opposite direction to the animation cels.

2. CHANGING SHAPE

So far you've been making cartoon characters that stay the same shape throughout the flipbook. By changing the shape or size of your cartoon characters, you can create some fun optical illusions.

Cartoon animators sometimes change the shape of cartoon characters to create different effects. For example, how could you animate a rubber ball so that it would look as if it were hitting the ground and then bouncing back up again? When animators want to show a bouncing ball hitting the ground, they draw the ball squished flat like a pancake. This technique simulates the force of gravity on the ball as it hits the ground. The ball gradually becomes a circle again as it bounces back up into the air.

You can also change the shape of a cartoon character to make it move. Creatures such as caterpillars and worms crawl along the ground by stretching the front of their body forward

then pulling the rest of their body so that it catches up. You can make your characters crawl by changing their shape.

The size of your cartoon characters can also be changed to create certain animation effects. For example, objects that are far away from us appear small in size. Objects that are closer to us appear to be bigger. Drawing your cartoon characters this way will give your scene the illusion of depth. This optical illusion is called perspective. By drawing your character a bit bigger in each successive drawing, you can make it look as if it is coming towards you. In this chapter, you will use this technique to make an airplane look as if it's flying right at you!

In this chapter you'll still be using stencils, but at certain points in the animation, you'll be re-drawing the character in a slightly different shape or size to create a new effect. Use a stencil as instructed.

BOUNCE A BALL

Imagine what a bouncing ball would look like in slow motion. An animated ball changes shape when it hits the ground to give it the illusion of bounce.

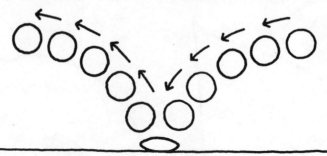

1 On the page nearest the cardboard, draw a line near the bottom edge of the pad. This will be the ground on which the ball will bounce. Put the next page down and trace the ground onto this page. Repeat this procedure until you have drawn the ground on about 30 pages.

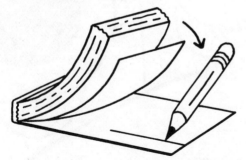

2 Tear a page off the front of your notepad. Draw a ball at least 1 cm (½ inch) wide on this page. This will be your first stencil.

3 Place a small bit of your ball on the cardboard towards the top of the open edge of the pad.

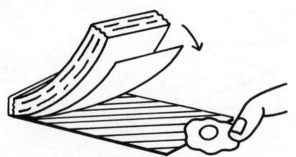

4 Place the back page on top and trace what you can see of the stencil.

5 Place your stencil over the last drawing and push the stencil into the pad about 4 mm and down 4 mm (about ¼ inch). Place the next page on top and trace what you can see of the stencil.

6 Repeat this procedure until the ball almost hits the ground.

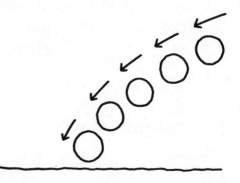

7 On the page where that ball will hit the ground, draw a new ball that looks like a flattened pancake. This is how animators simulate the force of the ball hitting the ground.

8 Place your stencil on top of the flattened ball. Push the stencil up in the opposite direction about 4 mm and into the pad about 4 mm. Place the next page on top and trace the ball.

9 Repeat this procedure until the ball is at about the same height that it entered the pad.

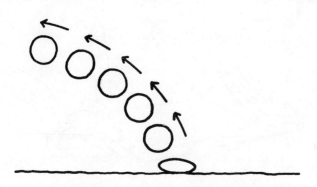

10 Flip the pages. Your ball will fly onto the page and gain speed as it falls. When it hits the ground, it will bounce and fly off quickly towards the centre of the pad.

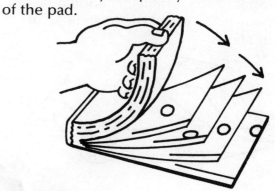

SQUISH AND STRETCH

We saw in the last flipbook that when a character hits the ground, the force of the impact squishes it flat. When a character is falling through the air, animators stretch it out. You can use squish and stretch to give your characters a feeling of weight and bounce.

1 On the page nearest the cardboard, draw a line near the bottom edge of the pad. Put the next page down and trace the ground onto this page. Repeat this procedure until you have the ground on about 30 pages.

2 Tear four pages off the front of your pad. Trace or draw the four versions of the character shown below, one character on each page. Copy the number under each drawing. These drawings will be your stencils.

#1   #2   #3   #4

3 Using stencil 1, place just a small bit of the bottom of the character on the cardboard. Your character should be placed towards the top of the open edge of the pad as shown.

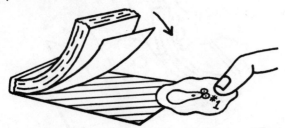

4 Place the back page on top and trace what you can see of the stencil.

5 Place your stencil over the last drawing and push it into the pad about 2 mm and down 2 mm. Place the next page on top of the stencil and trace it.

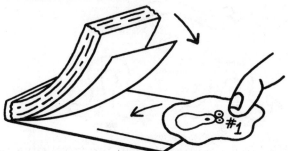

6 Repeat this procedure until the bottom of the character almost touches the ground.

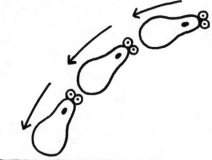

7 Place stencil 2 so that the bottom of the character is lying flat on the ground. Place the next page on top and trace the stencil.

8 Put stencil 3 on top of the last drawing. Don't move the stencil. Place the next page on top and trace the stencil.

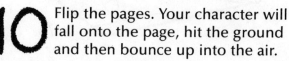

9 Place stencil 4 over the last drawing. Push the character up 2 mm and twist it in 2 mm towards the centre of the pad. Place the next page on top and trace the stencil. Repeat this procedure until the character has disappeared into the centre of the pad.

10 Flip the pages. Your character will fall onto the page, hit the ground and then bounce up into the air.

DO THE CATERPILLAR CRAWL

You can use the squish and stretch technique to make a caterpillar crawl along the ground.

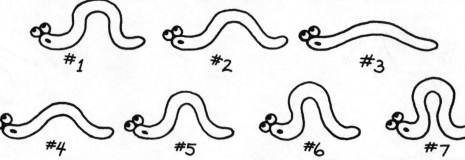

#1   #2   #3

#4   #5   #6   #7

1 On the page nearest the cardboard backing, draw a line near the bottom edge of the pad. Put the next page down and trace the ground onto this page. Repeat this procedure until you have drawn the ground on about 30 pages.

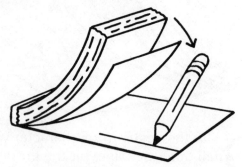

2 Tear seven pages off the front of your pad. Trace or draw the seven versions of the caterpillar shown above. Copy the number under each drawing. These will be your stencils.

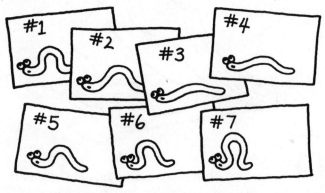

#1   #2   #3   #4

#5   #6   #7

3 On the page nearest the cardboard, place stencil 1 on the ground line so that the entire caterpillar can be seen and the back portion is touching the open edge of the pad. Place the next page over top and trace the stencil, including the #1.

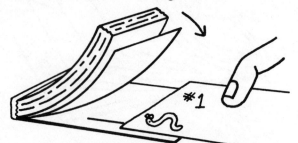

#1

TIP *The secret behind the caterpillar crawl is that one half of the caterpillar stays still while the other half moves. Line up stencils 1, 2 and 3 so that the tail of the caterpillar stays in place and the front part of the caterpillar stretches forward.*

#1

#2

#3

4 Place stencil 2 over the last drawing so that the tails of the two caterpillars are directly on top of each other. Don't move your stencil.

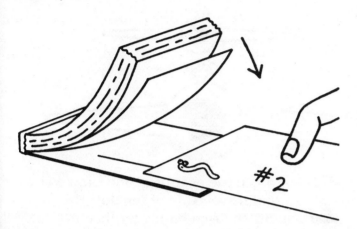

5 Place the next page over top and trace the stencil. Repeat this procedure with stencil 3, keeping the tails lined up.

T I P

Now it's time to move your caterpillar's tail section so that it catches up with the front section. The tail section moves forward in stencils 4, 5, 6 and 7.

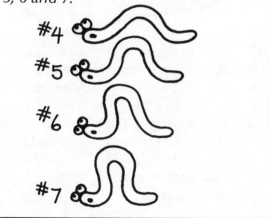

6 Place stencil 4 over the last drawing so that the heads of the two caterpillars are directly on top of each other. Don't move your stencil. Place the next page on top and trace the stencil. Repeat this procedure with stencils 5, 6 and 7.

7 Now go back and repeat steps 3 through 6 until the caterpillar crawls out of sight near the glue binding of your notepad.

8 When you flip the pages, your caterpillar will crawl across the page. Erase the stencil numbers from the pages of your flipbook.

AN AIRPLANE FLIES TOWARDS YOU

It's easy to animate an airplane flying towards you. The parts of the plane will gradually grow bigger as the airplane gets closer and closer.

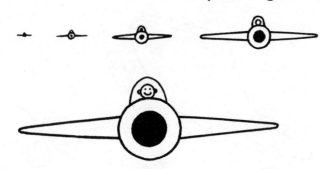

1 On the page nearest the cardboard, draw a tiny dot in the middle of the page near the open end of the pad. You'll make this dot grow bigger.

2 Put down the next page and draw a circle around the outside of the dot. The circle should be just a bit bigger than the dot.

3 Put down the next page and draw a slightly bigger circle around the first circle. Repeat this procedure until the edges of the circle touch and go off the edges of the page.

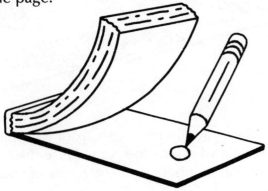

4 Flip the pages. It will look like your circle is coming towards you. This is the body of the airplane. Now go to the back of the pad where the small dot is, and add two tiny wings to the dot. Put down the next page and draw two slightly larger wings around the first two wings. Repeat this procedure until the wings disappear off the edges of the page.

5 Let's add a cockpit to the plane. Go back to the dot and add a tiny dot on top of it. Put down the next page and draw a half circle around the new dot. Repeat this procedure until the half circle disappears off the edges of the page.

6 Now go back and add the pilot's head. Flip the pages to where there is enough space in the half circle to fit the pilot's head. In the first drawing, the head should be just a dot. Put down the next page and make the circle grow bigger. Repeat this procedure until the cockpit disappears off the edges of the page. Then go back and add eyes, ears, nose and mouth to your head drawings.

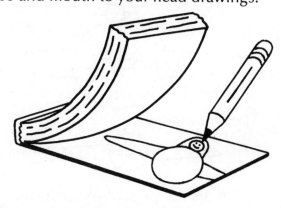

7 Go to the back of the pad. Flip in two or three pages. Draw a dot in the middle of the small circle in the middle of the plane's body. Put down the next page and draw a slightly bigger circle around the first circle. Shade in this second circle with your pencil. Repeat this procedure until the inner circle leaves the edges of the page.

8 Flip the pages. Your airplane will fly towards you.

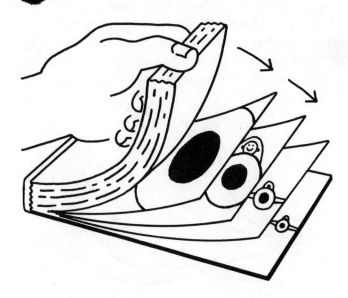

In the last flipbook you made your airplane appear to get closer by starting with small drawings and making them larger and larger. How do you think you can animate an airplane flying away? Right, you'll start with large drawings and make them smaller and smaller. You can use the same pad that you used for the previous airplane flipbook.

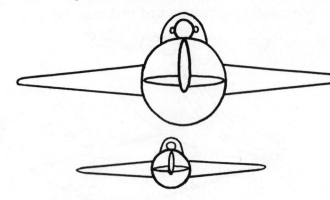

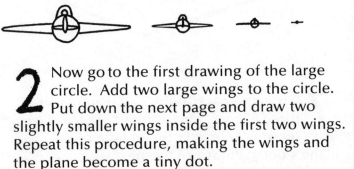

1 Start at the last page of your airplane flipbook where the body of your airplane has filled the entire page of the flipbook. Put the next page down. Draw a slightly smaller circle on this page. Put the next page down and draw a slightly smaller circle inside the first circle. Repeat this procedure until the circle shrinks to a tiny dot in the middle of the page.

2 Now go to the first drawing of the large circle. Add two large wings to the circle. Put down the next page and draw two slightly smaller wings inside the first two wings. Repeat this procedure, making the wings and the plane become a tiny dot.

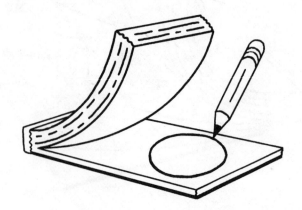

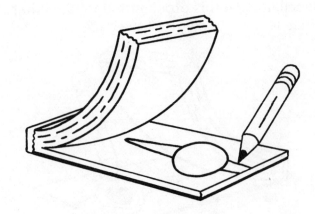

3 Let's add a cockpit to the plane. Go back to the first drawing of the large circle and add a half circle to the top of the large circle. Put down the next page and trace a slightly smaller half circle inside the first half circle. Repeat this procedure until the cockpit and the plane become a tiny dot.

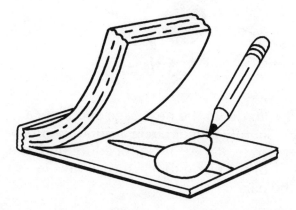

4 Flip the pages to the page where there is enough space in the half circle for the pilot's head. Draw a circle for the pilot's head in the cockpit. Put down the next page and draw a slightly smaller circle inside the first circle. Repeat this procedure until the cockpit and the plane become a tiny dot. Then go back and add ears to the drawings of your pilot's head.

5 Go back to the first large circle. Draw a set of three tail wings in the middle of the plane's body. The tail wings should touch the edges of the circle that makes up the plane's body. Put down the next page and draw three slightly smaller tail wings inside the first set of tail wings. Repeat this procedure until the three tail wings and the plane become a tiny dot.

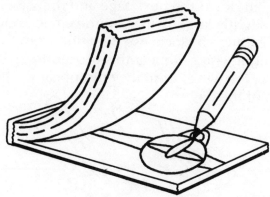

6 When you flip the pages, your airplane should fly away from you.

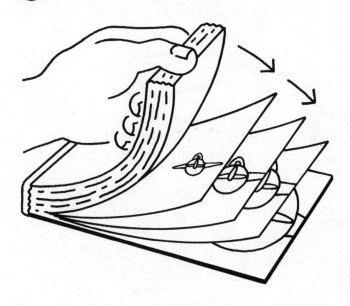

Fancy Flying

Now that you've made your plane fly towards you and away from you, you can try some acrobatic flying. You'll use the same techniques you used on the previous airplane flipbook, with a new twist. Use a new pad for this flipbook.

1 On the page nearest the cardboard backing, draw a tiny dot in the middle of the page near the open end of the pad. You'll make this dot grow bigger. Put down the next page and draw a circle around the outside of the dot. The circle should be just a bit bigger than the dot.

2 Put down the next page and draw a slightly bigger circle around the first circle. Repeat this procedure until the edges of the circle touch and go off the edges of the page.

3 This is the body of the airplane. Go to the back of the pad where the small dot is and add two tiny wings to the dot.

4 Put down the next page and draw two slightly larger wings on the circle about 2 mm in a clockwise direction from the first set of wings. Repeat this procedure, turning the wings until they disappear off the edges of the page.

5 Flip the pages. Your plane should be spinning and flying towards you. Add a cockpit to the plane. Go back to the dot and add a tiny dot on top of it. Put down the next page and draw a slightly bigger half circle 2 mm in a clockwise direction from the tiny dot. Repeat this procedure until the half circle disappears off the edges of the page.

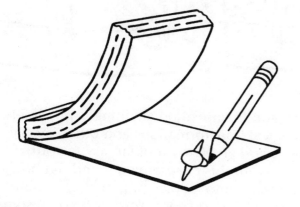

6 Go back and add the pilot's head in the cockpit.

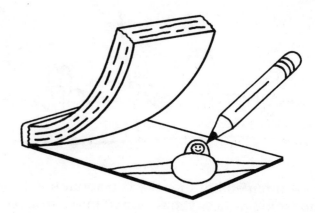

7 Go to the back of the pad. Flip in two or three pages. Draw a dot in the middle of the small circle in the middle of the plane's body. Put down the next page and draw a slightly bigger circle around the first circle. Shade in this second circle with your pencil. Repeat this procedure until the inner circle leaves the edges of the page.

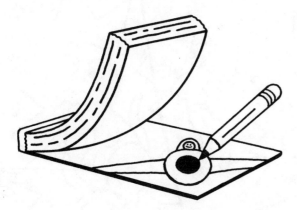

8 Flip the pages. Your airplane will fly towards you, spinning around as it flies.

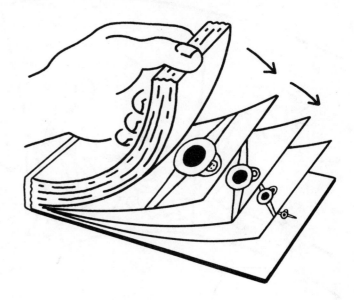

3. SPECIAL EFFECTS

Do you remember the fairy tale about the handsome prince who is turned into a frog by a witch? This change from prince to frog is called a magical transformation or metamorphosis. Can you imagine how you could animate this metamorphosis? Take a look at the short animated sequence below of a kid using a magic wand to change a frog into a dinosaur. In animation anything is possible!

Magical transformations and other special effects add an element of fantasy to your flipbook. In this chapter you'll find out how to turn a seed into a flower and make a rabbit appear out of nowhere. You can also try some special effects, such as having a spider spin a web or make a skateboarder do stunts.

MAKE A FACE APPEAR

In this flipbook, you'll learn the technique to make a face appear out of thin air.

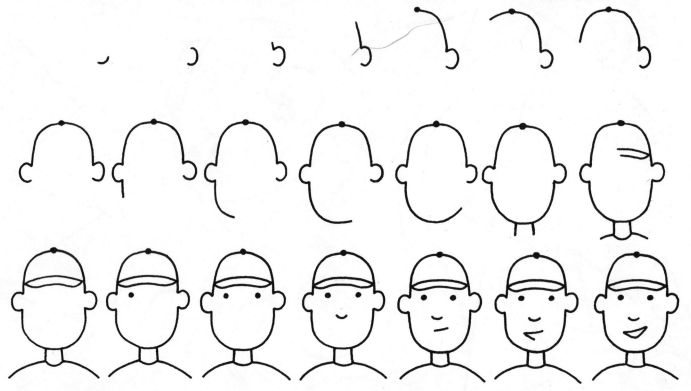

1 Tear a page off the front of your notepad. Draw a simple cartoon face on the right-hand side of this page. Don't add too much detail. This will be your stencil.

2 Place the stencil on the cardboard backing of the pad. The edges of the stencil page should line up with the edges of the cardboard backing as shown.

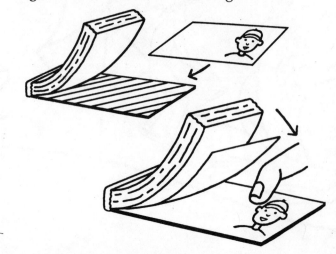

3 Place the back page on top and trace only a 2-mm (about the width of a toothpick) piece of the character's ear.

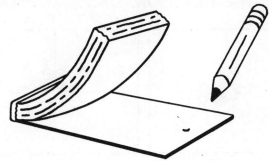

4 Place your stencil over the last drawing. Make sure the stencil is lined up directly over the last page. Place the next page on top and trace the same 2-mm piece of the character's ear. Then trace a bit more of the character's ear so that the line grows.

5 On each page, trace what you have drawn before and add a little bit more. The line should grow gradually (2 mm) on each page. Repeat this procedure until all the outside of the head can be seen on the page.

6 Place the stencil directly over your last drawing. Now you can add part of the character's face. Trace the outline of the character's head and trace one eye.

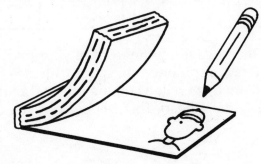

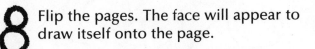

7 Place your stencil on top of this last drawing and repeat the procedure. This time trace both eyes. Repeat this procedure until the eyes, nose and mouth appear.

8 Flip the pages. The face will appear to draw itself onto the page.

SPIN A WEB

A spider builds its web slowly, strand by strand, gradually spinning an intricate web. You can animate this web-building procedure in a flipbook.

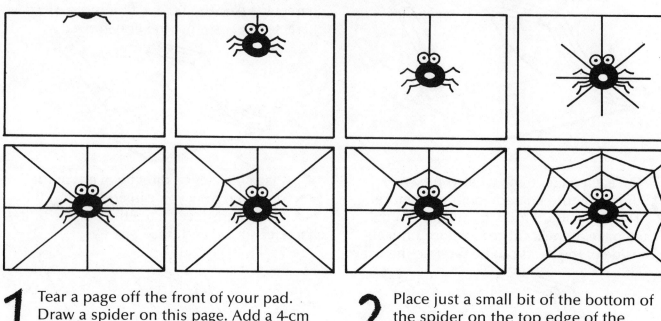

1 Tear a page off the front of your pad. Draw a spider on this page. Add a 4-cm (2-inch) web line coming out of the top of the spider's head. This will be your stencil.

2 Place just a small bit of the bottom of the spider on the top edge of the cardboard backing of your pad.

3 Place the back page on top and trace what you can see of the stencil.

4 Place your stencil over the last drawing and push the stencil down about 2 mm. Place the next page on top of the stencil and trace it. Repeat this procedure until all of the spider reaches the middle of the page.

5 Now you can start to spin your web. Draw seven 2-mm lines fanning out in all directions from the spider's body. These lines will shoot out and form the basic structure of the web.

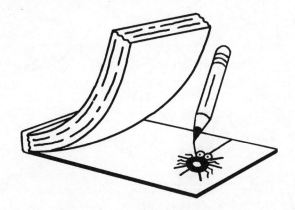

6 Place the next page on top of your stencil and trace the spider. Now trace the web lines and add another 2 mm to the lines. Repeat this procedure until your web lines have reached the edges of the page.

7 Put down the next page and trace the spider and web lines. Now add curved lines to join the web lines together. These curved lines will make circles around the spider. Add one more curved line on each new page. When you have completed one circle, draw another curved line farther away from the spider.

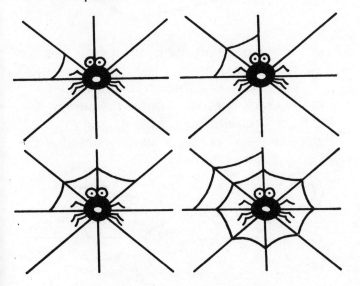

8 When you flip the pages, your spider will float down onto the page with its web line. When the spider reaches the middle of the page, more web lines will shoot out in all directions, until an intricately patterned web is created.

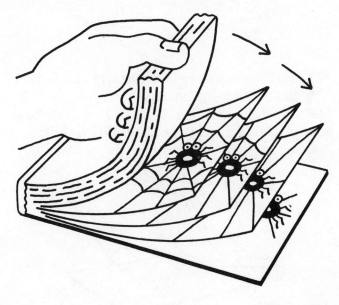

HATCH A CHICK

It's very exciting to watch a baby chick hatch out of an egg. First the chick breaks the egg with its beak, then the egg cracks open and the chick hops out. Try hatching your own baby chick in a flipbook.

1 On the page nearest to the cardboard backing, draw a large egg on its side.

2 Place the next page on top and carefully trace the entire egg. Now add a tiny 2-mm crack line in the egg at the top edge.

3 Put the next page on top and carefully trace your egg again. Then trace the crack line adding another 2 mm line to it. Repeat this procedure until the crack line reaches the other side of the egg.

4 Tear a page off the front of your pad. Lay this page over your last drawing of the egg. Trace just the left half of the egg and the crack line. Then move the stencil page and trace the right half of the egg and the crack line. You now have two separate halves for your stencils.

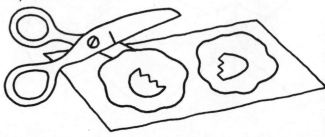

5 Take the left half of the egg stencil and line it up directly on top of the last drawing of the egg. Now twist the stencil to the left 2 mm and push it down 2 mm.

6 Put the next page down and trace what you can see. Place the stencil on top of the last drawing and twist the stencil to the left 2 mm and down 2 mm. Repeat this procedure until the left half of the egg has disappeared off the bottom of the page.

7 Go back to the last drawing of the full egg and repeat this procedure with the right half of the egg, twisting it to the right. Continue until the right half of the egg has disappeared off the bottom of the page.

8 Tear another page off the front of your pad. Draw a baby chick on this page small enough to fit inside the egg. This will be your new stencil.

9 At the last drawing of the full egg, place the chick stencil on top so that the baby chick is inside the egg. Put the next page down. Trace what you can see of the baby chick in the space between the two halves of the broken egg. Take the chick stencil out and place it directly on top of the last drawing of the baby chick. Put the next page down and trace what you can see of the new stencil between the broken halves of the egg.

10 Repeat this procedure until all of the baby chick is visible and the two halves of the egg have fallen off the bottom of the page.

Flip the pages. The egg will crack open and fall apart to reveal a baby chick.

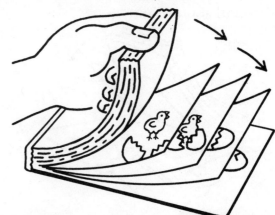

MAKE A FLOWER GROW

A flower starts out as a tiny seed in the ground. Gradually it pokes its head out of the ground and grows towards the sun. You can use animation to make a flower grow.

1 On the page nearest to the cardboard backing, draw a line near the bottom of the pad. This will be the ground line out of which your plant will grow. Put the next page down and trace the ground onto this page. Repeat this procedure until you have drawn the ground on about 30 pages.

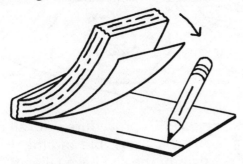

2 Tear a page off the front of your pad. Draw a bud and stem about 5 cm (2 inches) long like the one below. This will be your stencil.

3 Go to the back page of your pad. Place your stencil at the bottom of this page so that the tip of the bud is poking out of the ground about 2 mm.

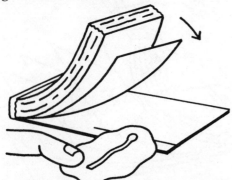

4 Place the next page on top and trace what you can see of the bud above the ground line.

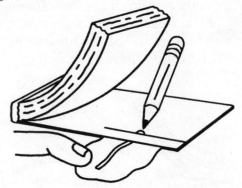

5 Place your stencil on top of the last drawing and push it up 2 mm. Place the next page on top and trace what you can see of the bud and stem above the ground line. Repeat this procedure until all of the bud and stem are seen above the ground line.

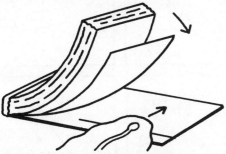

6 Now make the bud and stem become a flower. Trace the stem and add two tiny bumps on the sides of the stem. These bumps will gradually become the leaves of the flower. Draw a tiny line in the top of the bud. This line will grow gradually and the bud will split open.

7 Put the next page down and trace the stem. Make the bumps larger and more leaf-shaped. Open the bud a tiny bit on each page.

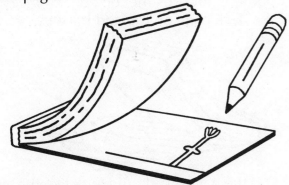

8 Place the next page down. Draw the leaves on the side of the stem a little bit bigger and add some vein lines. Change the two halves of the bud so that they look like the petals of a flower. Add two more petals between the halves. Add a black dot in between the halves.

9 Gradually your bud will open and your plant will bloom. The two leaves on the sides of the stem will grow as well. Remember to make tiny changes to your flower between drawings, so that your animation is smooth.

10 Flip the pages. Your bud will poke its head out of the ground. When it reaches its full height, it will blossom into a flower with two leaves.

PRESTO! MAKE A RABBIT APPEAR

You don't have to be a magician to wave your magic wand and make a rabbit appear. Performing magic tricks is easy in a flipbook.

1 Tear a page off the front of your pad. Draw an arm and hand holding a wand about the size of the arm shown below. This will be your stencil.

2 Place the stencil in the middle of the cardboard backing so that the wand is pointing towards the top edge of the pad. Place the back page on top and trace the stencil.

3 Place your stencil over the last drawing and push the stencil to the right 2 mm and down 2 mm. Place the next page on top and trace the stencil. Repeat this procedure until the wand is pointing towards the open edge of the pad.

4 Flip the pages. It should look like the arm is coming down. Now you can bring the arm back up.

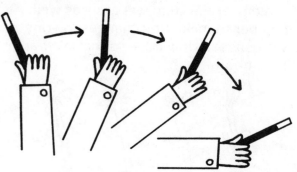

5 Place the stencil on top of the last drawing and push it up 2 mm and twist it to the left 2 mm. Put down the next page and trace the stencil. Repeat this procedure until the arm returns to its original position pointing to the top edge of the pad.

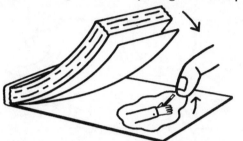

6 Go back to the drawing where the wand is pointing towards the open edge of the page. At the tip of the wand, draw a small star. Put the next page down and draw a bigger star around the first star. It is best if the stars are not the same shape.

7 Put the next page over the last drawing and draw a smaller star inside the biggest star. Put the next page down and draw a smaller star inside the last drawing.

8 Tear another page off the front of your pad. Draw a rabbit on this page. This will be your new stencil.

9 On the page with the biggest lightning flash, place your rabbit stencil over the flash. Put the next page on top and trace what you can see of the rabbit around the outside of the lightning flash. Repeat this procedure on each page until all of your rabbit can be seen.

10 Flip the pages. The arm with the wand will move downward. As the wand reaches the middle of the page, there will be a flash of lightning as a rabbit appears and the wand rises back up.

SKATEBOARDING

Have you tried stunts on a skateboard and ended up with bruised knees and elbows? It's a lot easier to perform amazing skateboarding stunts in a flipbook.

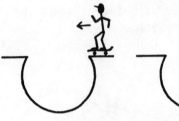

1 On the page nearest the cardboard backing, draw a curved ramp. Put the next page down and trace the ramp onto this page. Repeat this procedure until you have drawn the ramp on about 40 pages.

2 Tear a page off the front of your notepad. Draw a skateboard with a simple stick figure riding on it. Remember, the skateboarder must be small enough to fit inside your ramp. This will be your stencil.

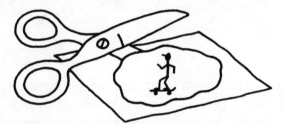

3 Place the tip of the front of the skateboarder on the cardboard. Make sure the wheels of the skateboard are touching the ground beside the ramp.

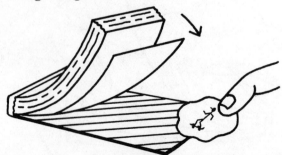

4 Place the next page on top and trace what you can see.

5 Place the stencil directly over your last drawing. Push the stencil into the pad about 2 mm. Place the next page down and trace what you can see. Repeat this procedure until the skateboarder has reached the edge of the ramp.

6 Now the skateboarder is ready to roll into the ramp. Push the skateboarder in 2 mm and then twist it down 2 mm. Make sure at least one of the wheels of the skateboard is touching the ramp. Place the next page down and trace what you can see. Repeat this procedure until the skateboarder is inside the ramp.

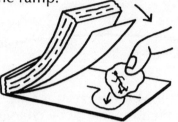

7 Twist the rider so that the skateboard moves forward along the ramp about 2 mm. Place the next page down and trace what you can see. Repeat this procedure until the skateboarder has ridden to the top of the left-hand side of the ramp.

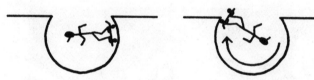

8 Make the skateboarder fly through the air to continue the loop-the-loop. Continue to twist it 2 mm in a circle. Repeat this procedure until the skateboarder reaches the right–hand side of the ramp again.

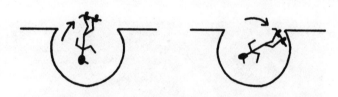

9 Continue to animate until the skateboarder reaches the left-hand side of the ramp again. When the skateboarder has reached the level part of the ramp, push the stencil into the pad about 2 mm. Repeat this procedure until the skateboarder has disappeared into the centre of the pad.

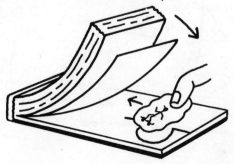

10 Flip the pages. Your skateboarder will ride onto the page, then perform an exciting loop-the-loop in the ramp. After one loop, the skateboarder will ride out of the ramp and out of sight.

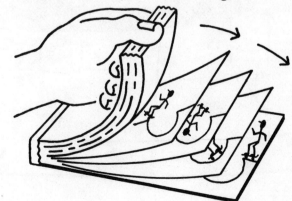

4. MORE FUN

In this chapter, you'll give your cartoon character some personality by changing its facial expressions, you'll go on a journey through outer space, and you'll learn how to make special personalized flipbooks that you can give as gifts.

In the flipbooks, "Blast off," "Journey through space" and "Touch down" you'll make a short movie made up of several shots. In real movies, every time the camera is moved to a new position it's called a new shot. Sometimes the new shot takes place in a totally different scene or setting. In the flipbook "Blast off" we see the first shot of a rocket taking off from earth. Then, we cut to a new shot in "Journey through space" where

the rocket flies through space. Finally, in "Touch down," the rocket appears in the final shot, where it lands on a distant planet. Try using different shots in your flipbook movies to make them longer and more interesting.

SMILE!

The next few projects can be combined to make a story about a fly landing on your character's nose. You'll need a notepad with at least 96 pages.

1 Tear a page off the front of your pad. Draw a simple cartoon head with only the ears, neck and nose on this page. This will be your stencil.

2 Place your stencil on the cardboard backing. Put the next page down and trace the head onto this page. Continue tracing the head on each page until you have drawn it on about 25 pages.

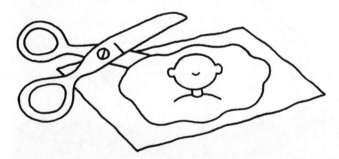

3 On the page nearest the cardboard, draw two curved lines on either side of the nose. It should look as if your character has its eyes closed.

4 Place the next page on top. Trace the two eye lines, but this time add a second line above the first two lines.

5 Draw in the eyes on your character, opening them a little more on each page as you go.

6 Now make your character smile. On the page nearest the cardboard, draw a dot under the nose. This dot will gradually grow into a curved mouth.

7 Place the next page down and draw a tiny line where the dot is. Place the next page on top and draw a slightly longer line. To make your character look happy, start to curve up the edges of the line until you have a nice big smile.

8 Flip the pages. Your character will open its eyes and break into a smile. Turn to the next activity and we'll make our character respond to another character.

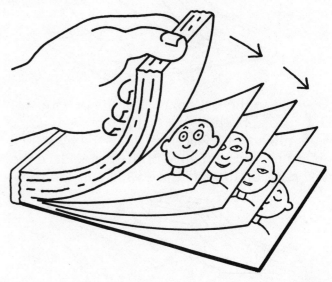

A FLY LANDS ON YOUR NOSE

What would your character do if a fly landed on its nose? Continue with the same pad and stencil that you used on the previous project.

1 Go to your last drawing of the face. Place the first stencil directly on top of the last drawing. Put the next page down and trace the head onto this page. Repeat this procedure until you have drawn the head on about 30 pages.

2 Tear a page off the front of your pad. Draw a tiny cartoon fly on this page. The fly should be about the size of the first character's nose. This will be your new stencil.

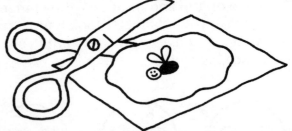

3 Go to the last drawing of the previous project (where the character's eyes are fully open). Place the tip of the fly stencil on top of the open edge of the page. Place the next page on top and trace what you can see.

4 Place the stencil directly on top of the last drawing. Push the stencil into the pad about 2 mm. Place the next page down and trace what you can see. Repeat this procedure until the fly has flown onto the page.

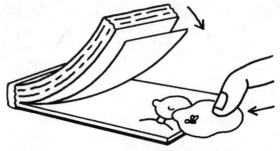

5 Continue moving your stencil 2 mm around the face so that the fly appears to fly around the left-hand side of the person's head. When it has reached the top of the head, have the fly float down to land on the nose.

6 Go back to the last drawing of the previous project where the eyes are fully open. Place the next page on top. Trace the character's eyeballs but move the pupils so that your character is looking at the fly. Repeat this procedure to the page where the fly lands on the character's nose.

7 Go back to the page where you left off the previous project. Place the next page down. Draw a slightly shorter line for the character's mouth. Place the next page down and draw an even shorter line. Repeat this procedure until you have a dot again.

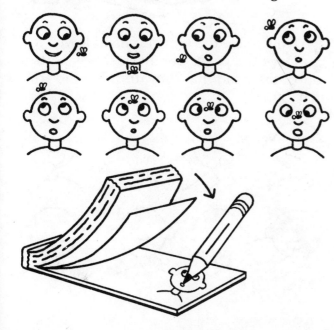

8 When you flip the pages, your character will open its eyes and break into a happy smile. Then a fly will fly around the character's head and land on its nose. The eyes of the character follow the flight of the fly. The expression on the character's face will change from happy to puzzled. Turn the page and we'll make our character shoo the fly away.

SHOO FLY

If a fly landed on your nose, your first impulse would be to shoo the fly away. Use the same pad and stencils that you used on the two previous projects.

1 Place the stencil on the last page of the previous project. Put the next page down and trace the head onto this page. Repeat this procedure until you have drawn the head on about 30 pages.

2 Tear a page off the front of your pad. Draw an arm about the size of the one shown below. This will be your third stencil.

3 Go to the last drawing of the previous project. Place the arm stencil so that the tip of the hand appears on the bottom edge of the pad. Put the next page down and trace what you can see. Repeat this procedure, twisting the stencil 2 mm up and 2 mm to the right each time until the hand is touching the character's nose.

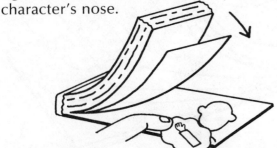

4 Now make the arm and hand lower and leave the page. Gently erase any parts of the head that show through the arm and hand.

5 Go back to the last drawing of the previous project. Place the next page down and trace the fly on the character's nose. Trace the fly on each page until the hand and arm touch the nose. Then place the stencil of your fly on the nose and push the stencil up 2 mm and to the right 2 mm. Place the next page down and trace what you can see. Repeat this procedure until the fly has flown off the page.

6 Go back to the last drawing of the previous project. Place the next page on top. Trace the character's eyeballs but move the pupils so that your character is looking at the fly. Place the next page down and trace the eyeballs again. Move the pupils so that they follow the flight of the fly. Repeat this procedure until the fly flies off the page.

7 Go back to the last drawing of the previous project. Place the next page down. Trace the circle of the character's mouth until the fly has flown off the page. Don't trace the mouth through the arm and hand. After the fly has flown off, gradually make your character smile.

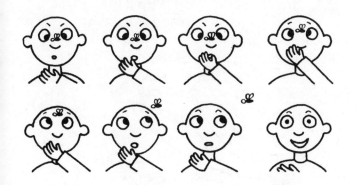

8 When you flip the pages of the entire pad, you'll have a story about a fly landing on your character's nose.

BLAST OFF!

By combining this project with the next two projects, you can explore outer space in a flipbook. You'll need a notepad with at least 96 pages for this flipbook adventure.

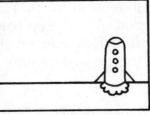
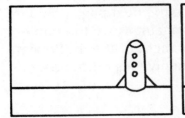
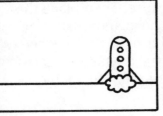
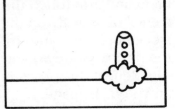

1 Draw a ground line on about 25 pages, as you did in step 1 of page 26.

2 Tear a page off the front of your pad. Draw a simple rocket on this page. This will be your stencil.

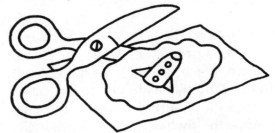

3 Place your stencil on the page that is nearest to the cardboard. The rocket should be resting on the ground. Place the next page on top and trace the rocket. Repeat this procedure for five pages.

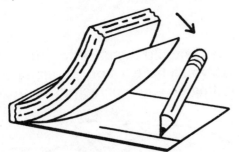

4 Place the stencil on top of the last drawing and push it up 2 mm. Place the next page on top and trace what you can see. Repeat this procedure until the rocket flies off the top edge of the pad.

5 Return to the first five drawings. Using an eraser, gently erase the part of the ground line that is showing through the middle of the rocket. On page two, draw a tiny bit of smoke coming out of the bottom of the rocket.

6 Place the next page down and draw a bigger cloud of smoke. The smoke can cover part of the body of the rocket. Add a little bit more smoke on each page until the rocket starts to blast off.

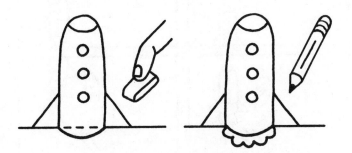

7 As the rocket lifts off, draw less and less smoke until it disappears. Erase any part of the rocket that is showing through the smoke. Now you can add a little bit of fire to the tail of the rising rocket. Make the flame different shapes and lengths on each page.

8 Flip the pages and watch your rocket blast off. Turn the page and we'll make the rocket fly through space!

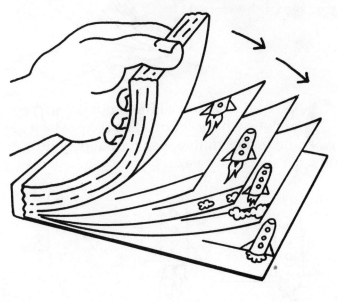

JOURNEY THROUGH SPACE

You've left earth far behind. Now make your rocket speed through space, passing a moon and a shooting star. Use the same pad you used on the previous project.

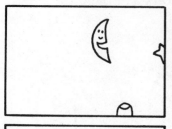

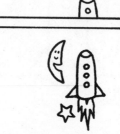

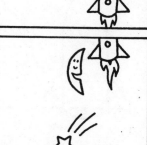

1 Go to the last drawing of the previous project (pages 68 to 69). Place the tip of your rocket stencil on this page so that the nose of the rocket enters the bottom edge of the pad. Place the next page on top and trace what you can see of the stencil.

2 Place your stencil on top of the last drawing and push it up 2 mm. Place the next page down and trace what you can see. Repeat this procedure until the rocket flies off the top edge of the pad.

3 Go back and add a little bit of fire to the tail of each rocket on each page. Make the flames different shapes and lengths on each successive page.

4 Tear a page off the front of your pad, draw a shooting star. Place the tip of the star on the last page of the rocket blasting off earth, as shown. Place the next page on top and trace what you can see of the star.

5 Place the shooting star directly on top of the last drawing and push it 2 mm in and twist it 2 mm down. Place the next page on top and trace what you can see. Repeat this procedure until the shooting star has passed behind the rocket and fallen off the bottom edge of the pad. When the rocket and the shooting star meet, do not trace the shooting star through the body of the rocket.

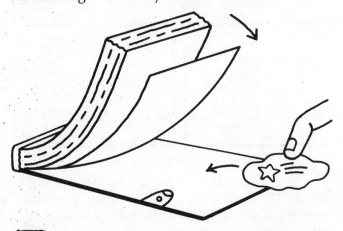

6 Go back to the first page where the rocket and shooting star are flying through space. Make a stencil of a half moon. Put the next page down and trace what you can see.

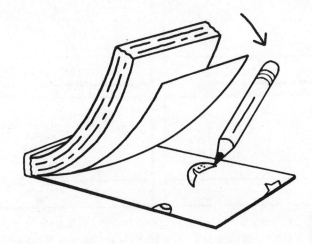

7 Place the next page on top and trace the half moon. Repeat this procedure until the moon is on every page. Stop when the spaceship and shooting star have left the page. Do not trace the half moon through the body of the rocket or the shooting star.

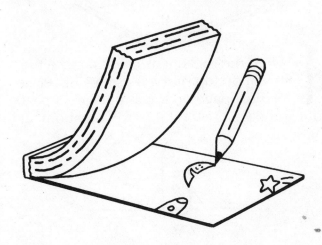

8 Flip the pages. The spaceship will fly onto the page and pass a shooting star and a moon, then fly off the top edge of the pad. Turn the page and we'll continue the adventure by making the rocket land on a distant planet.

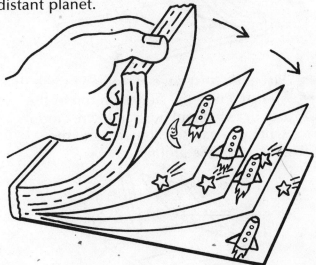

TOUCH DOWN

To complete the story of your rocket's journey, have it land on a planet. Use the same pad that you used on the two previous rocket flipbooks.

 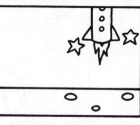 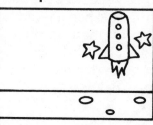 

1 Go to the last page of the rocket flying through outer space. Place the next page on top, and draw a line and three craters near the bottom of the pad. Draw the ground line and craters on about 30 pages.

2 Go back to the last page of the rocket flying through outer space. Place the bottom tip of your rocket stencil on the page, so that it is coming in from the top edge of the pad.

3 Place the next page on top and trace the stencil. Place the stencil on top of the last drawing and push it down 2 mm. Trace what you can see. Repeat until the rocket lands on the ground.

4 When the rocket has landed, place the stencil on top of the last drawing. Place the next page on top and trace. Repeat until you have drawn the rocket on about 10 pages.

5 Use an eraser to gently erase any of the ground line that is showing through the body of the rocket.

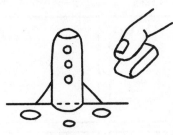

6 Go back and add a little bit of fire to the tail of each falling rocket. Make the flames different shapes and lengths on each successive page.

7 When the rocket lands, draw a tiny bit of smoke coming out of the bottom of the rocket. Place the next page down and draw a bigger cloud of smoke. The smoke can cover part of the body of the rocket.

8 Add a little bit more smoke on each page. After four pages, start to draw less and less smoke until the smoke disappears. Erase any part of the rocket that is showing through the smoke.

9 Go back to the first page of the rocket landing. Draw two stars on this page. This will be the sky. Place the next page on top and trace the two stars. Repeat this procedure until the two stars are on every page. Don't trace the two stars through the body of the rocket.

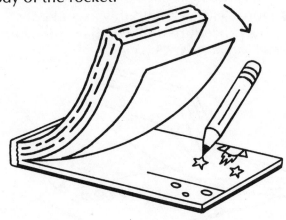

10 Flip the pages of the entire pad. You should see a short movie with three different scenes. The rocket should blast off, pass a moon and land on the surface of a faraway planet. What do you think the next scene could be?

HAPPY BIRTHDAY

You can use your new flipbook techniques to create gifts and cards that really talk. Try making this Happy Birthday flipbook for a friend's birthday.

1 Tear a page off the front of your pad. Print the word "Happy" on this page. This will be your first stencil. First you'll make the word "Happy" slide onto the page.

2 Go to the back of the pad. Place the tip of the "H" in the word "Happy" on the cardboard. Place the edge so that it is close to the top edge of the pad. Place the next page on top and trace what you can see.

3 Place the stencil directly over your last drawing. Push the stencil into the pad about 2 mm. Place the next page down and trace what you can see. Repeat this procedure until all of the word "Happy" has appeared on the page.

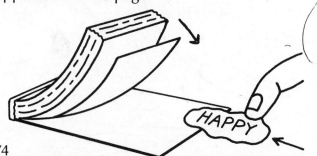

4 Place the next page on top and trace the word "Happy" onto this page. Repeat this procedure until you have the word "Happy" on at least 25 pages.

5 Tear another page off the front of your pad. Print the word "Birthday" on this page. This will be your second stencil.

6 Go back to the page where the entire word "Happy" appeared on the page. Place the tip of the "B" in "Birthday" on the page. The word "Birthday" will gradually slide onto the page under the word "Happy." Place the next page on top and trace what you can see.

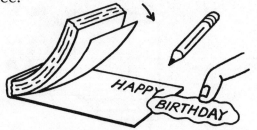

7 Place the second stencil directly over your last drawing. Push the stencil into the pad about 2 mm. Place the next page down and trace what you can see. Repeat this procedure until all of the word "Birthday" has appeared on the page.

8 When you flip the pages, the word "Happy" will slide onto the page, then the word "Birthday" slides on underneath it. Now add your friend's name to the flipbook. Go to the page where the entire phrase "Happy Birthday" first appears.

9 Under "Happy Birthday," print the first letter of your friend's name. Place the next page on top and trace the first letter of your friend's name and then add the second letter. Repeat this procedure until all of your friend's name appears on the page.

10 Flip the pages and you've got a personalized flipbook. If you like, you can make a birthday cake appear at the bottom of the page using the techniques that you learned on pages 48 to 49.

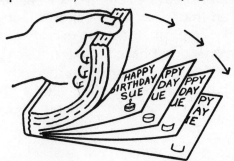

5. EARLY MOTION-PICTURE DEVICES

So far, you've been using flipbooks as a method of making cartoon characters move. In this chapter, you'll use some simple motion-picture devices to animate your characters. These motion-picture devices were invented more than 150 years ago to test out a theory, called "persistence of vision." Here's how it works.

When you flip the pages of one of your flipbooks, your eyes blend all the pictures together so that it looks as if your cartoon character is moving. This blending of pictures is called persistence of vision, and it was discovered in 1824 by Peter Mark Roget. Roget discovered that when we are shown many slightly different pictures very quickly in a row, our eyes don't have time to notice the spaces between the pictures. In the split second that it takes our eyes to send a message to our brain about one picture, we

are already seeing the next picture. Our eyes superimpose, or pile, one picture on top of another, so that we are tricked into seeing motion.

Scientists were very excited about Roget's ideas, and they began building moving-picture machines to test the theory of persistence of vision. In this chapter, you'll learn how to make some of these early motion-picture devices, such as the phenakistoscope and zoetrope—machines that create animation using a spinning wheel. Then you can move on to the final challenge of making a praxinoscope—a device that makes animated movement with mirrors. Start off by making the thaumatrope on the next page. The thaumatrope was one of the first moving-picture devices—it blends two pictures together.

THE THAUMATROPE

A thaumatrope is a small spinning disc with two strings attached to it. It was invented in 1825 by Dr. John Ayrton Paris. The word "thaumatrope" means "a turning marvel." When you spin a thaumatrope, two pictures are flashed quickly in front of your eyes, blending them together to make one picture.

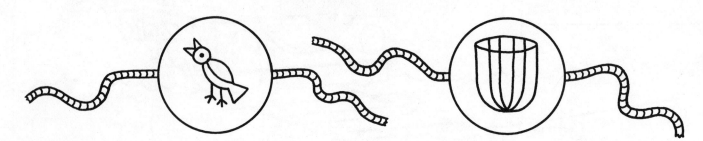

You'll need:
a pencil
a small cup
scissors
a piece of Bristol board or cardboard
string
sticky tape
white paper

1 Trace around the cup to make a circle on the Bristol board or cardboard. Cut out the circle.

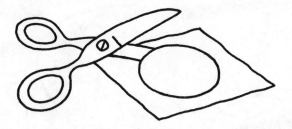

2 Cut two pieces of string 25 cm (10 inches) in length. Tape the pieces of string near the outside edges of the circle.

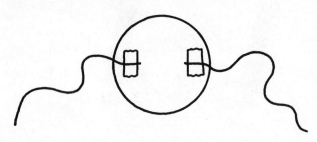

3 Trace the Bristol board circle twice on your white drawing paper. Cut out the two paper circles.

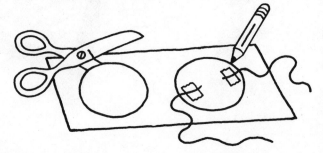

4 Decide what picture you would like to draw. If you need some ideas for your thaumatrope picture, have a look at the pictures on this page. Draw one picture on one of your white paper circles with your pencil.

5 Draw the other part of the picture on the second white paper circle.

6 Now make two rolls of sticky tape and attach one picture to one side of the cardboard circle.

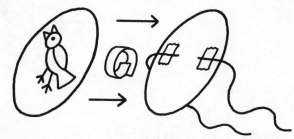

7 Tape the second picture to the other side of the cardboard circle. This picture must be upside-down to the picture on the front of the cardboard circle.

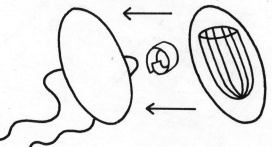

8 Now hold the thaumatrope by the two pieces of string. Roll the string between your fingers and the thaumatrope will begin to rotate, blending the two pictures together.

THE PHENAKISTOSCOPE

The first motion-picture machine was invented in 1832 by Joseph Plateau. Plateau called his invention the phenakistoscope, meaning "an instrument for observing a trick or illusion." Plateau made this device to show how our eyes blend pictures together. You can amaze your friends with your own phenakistoscope.

You'll need:
a pencil
a piece of white paper
scissors
a piece of black Bristol board
glue

a ruler
a fine black felt-tip pen
a push pin
a mirror
a light

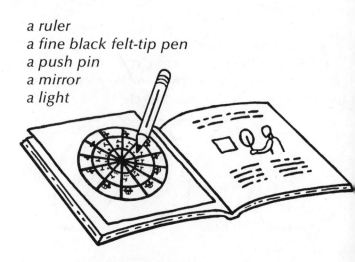

1 Trace or draw the phenakistoscope disk on page 82 onto your white paper. Outline the pictures and lines with a fine black marker.

2 Glue the white paper onto the black Bristol board. Use a small amount of glue and spread it around so that all edges of the paper will be glued down. Let the glue dry.

3 Cut out the circle with your scissors.

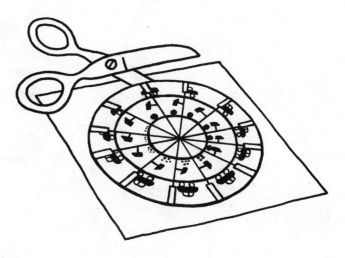

4 At the 12 points where the line meets the edge of the circle cut out the narrow slits 2 mm (⅛ inch) wide and 2 cm (¾ inch) into the circle.

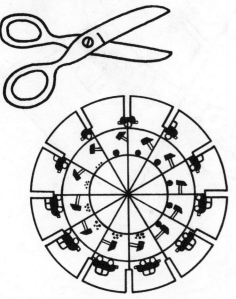

5 Mount the disk on a pencil by pushing a push pin through the centre of the white circle into the eraser on the end of your pencil.

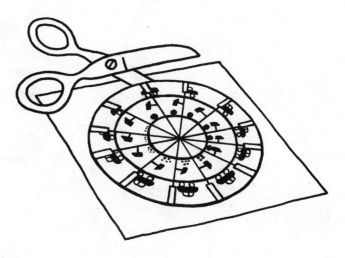

81

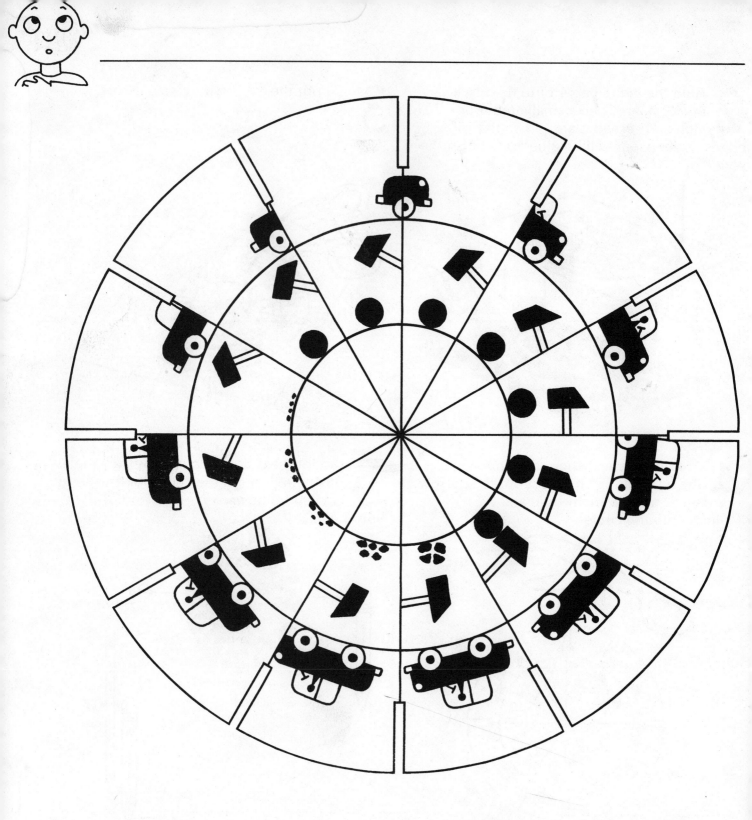

This page may be photocopied for personal or group use. **Animation** © 1991 by Patrick Jenkins, Addison-Wesley Publishing Company, Inc

6 Hold the phenakistoscope in front of a mirror with the white disk facing the mirror. Look through the slits, keeping both of your eyes open. Now spin the disk. Your car will drive across the pie-shaped segments and the hammer will break the round stone. Shine a light on the side of the disk where the drawings are. This will make the animation easier to see.

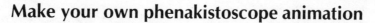

Make your own phenakistoscope animation

If you'd like to make your own phenakistoscope images, trace the disk on page 82 without tracing the pictures. This time fill in your own animated sequence. Remember that you only have 12 panels to complete your animation. Because the phenakistoscope is a spinning disk, it is best to make your animation a visual loop, that is a sequence of images where the last image joins up with the first to make a story without an end. Test your animation in the mirror. Once you are happy with the animation, outline the images in black marker.

THE ZOETROPE

Another motion-picture machine invented in the 1830s was the zoetrope, or "the wheel of life." The zoetrope was invented in 1834 by William Horner, and it was a very popular toy in its day. Like the phenakistoscope, the zoetrope is easy to make.

You'll need:
a pencil
white paper
a fine black felt-tip marker
glue
a piece of black Bristol board
scissors
a ruler
stapler
sticky tape
a push pin
a button
a light

1 Trace the circle on page 85 onto a piece of white paper. Outline the lines and balls with a fine black marker.

2 Glue the white paper onto the black Bristol board. Use a small amount of glue and spread it around so that all edges of the paper will be glued down. Let the glue dry.

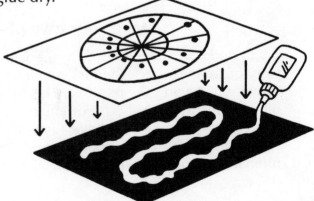

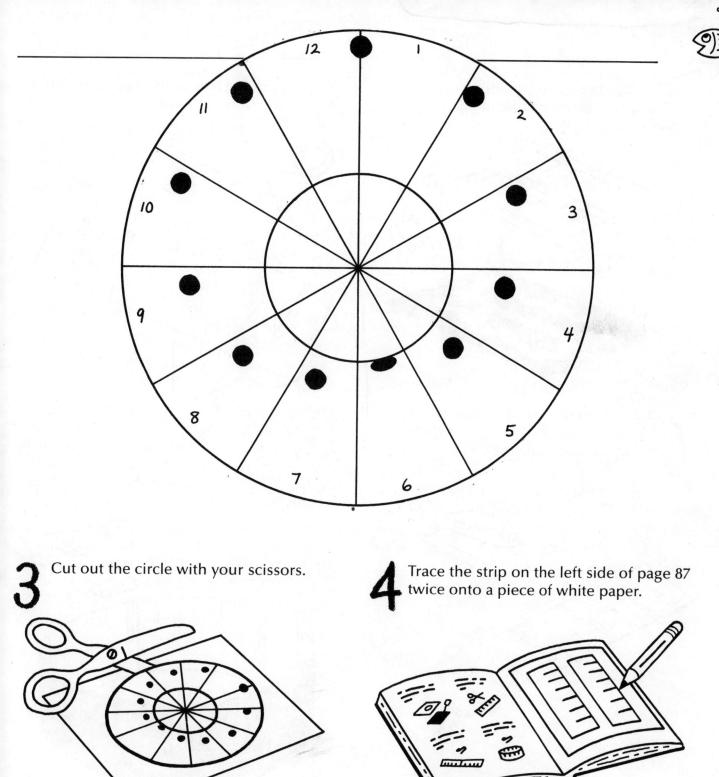

3 Cut out the circle with your scissors.

4 Trace the strip on the left side of page 87 twice onto a piece of white paper.

Animation © 1991 by Patrick Jenkins, Addison-Wesley Publishing Company, Inc.

5 Glue the white paper onto the black Bristol board and let the glue dry.

6 Cut out the two strips, then cut out the narrow slits in the strips.

7 Overlap the two strips so that at least 2.5 cm (1 inch) on each end overlaps. Staple the strips together.

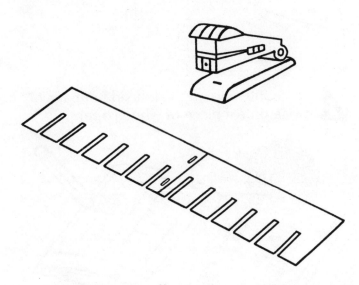

8 Take the strip with the slits and bend it so that it forms a circle. Overlap the two end pieces so that at least 2.5 cm (1 inch) on each end overlaps. Staple these two ends together. The black surface should be on the outside.

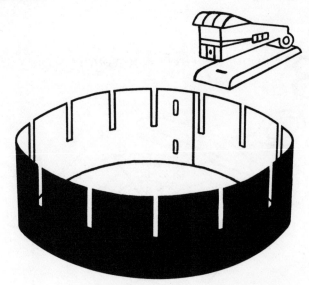

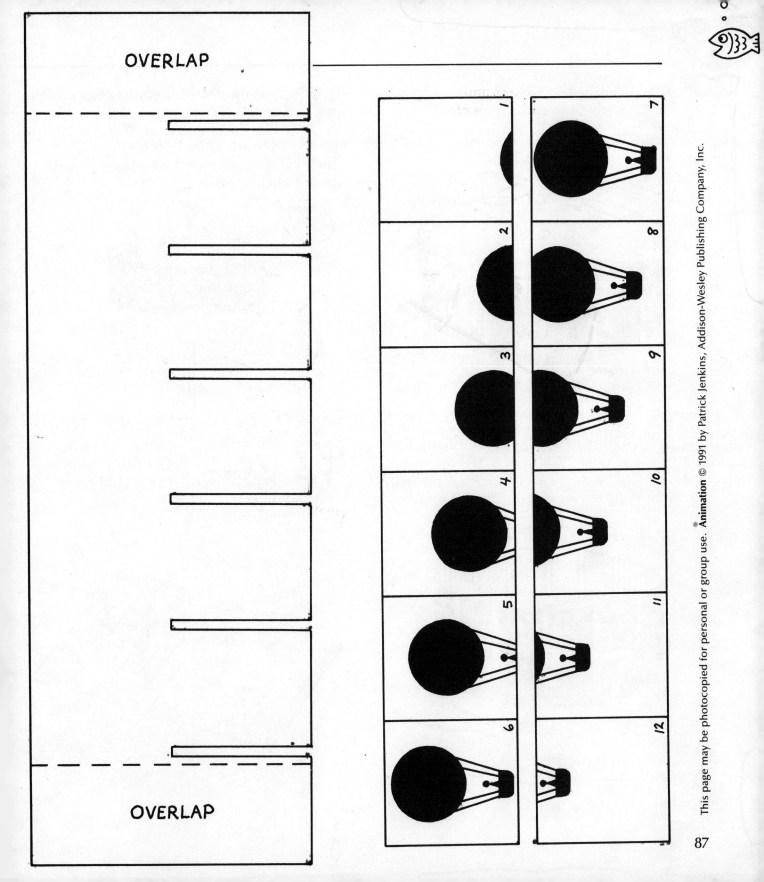

OVERLAP

OVERLAP

9 Tape the black circle to the strip with the slits.

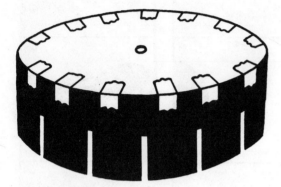

10 Push a pin through the centre of the circle in the bottom of the drum. Place a button over the point of the pin. The button will make the drum easier to spin. Push the pin into the end of a pencil where the eraser is.

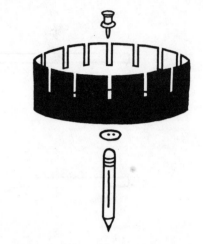

11 Hold the zoetrope in your hand by the pencil and spin it. If it doesn't spin easily, your push pin is pushed too far into the eraser. Pull the pin out a tiny bit.

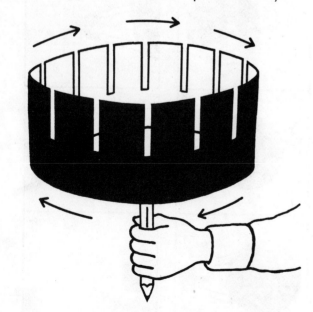

12 Trace the animation strips of the hot-air balloon on page 87 onto a piece of white paper. Outline and fill in the balloons with a black marker.

13 Cut out the two animation strips. Place panel number 6 beside panel number 7 and tape the two strips together. Put your tape on the back of the strip so that it doesn't show.

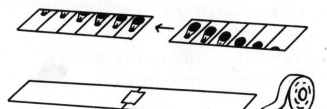

14 Place the strip in the zoetrope cylinder. Spin the drum and look through the slits. Your balloon will fly up or float down depending on which way you spin the zoetrope drum. Hold your zoetrope cylinder under a light to make the animation show up better. Try making the strip of the running figure on this page.

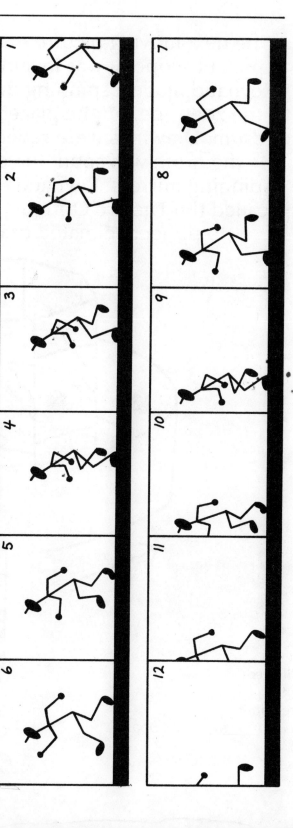

THE PRAXINOSCOPE

The next moving-picture machine invented was called the praxinoscope. It was invented in 1877 by Emile Reynaud. Reynaud made a spinning drum, similar to the one used in the zoetrope, but he placed mirrors in the middle of the drum. Drawings were reflected in the mirrors, and when the drum was spun, the drawings came to life in the spinning mirrors. Reynaud opened the first movie theatre, called the Theatre Optique, in 1892, using a praxinoscope to project animated drawings on a movie screen.

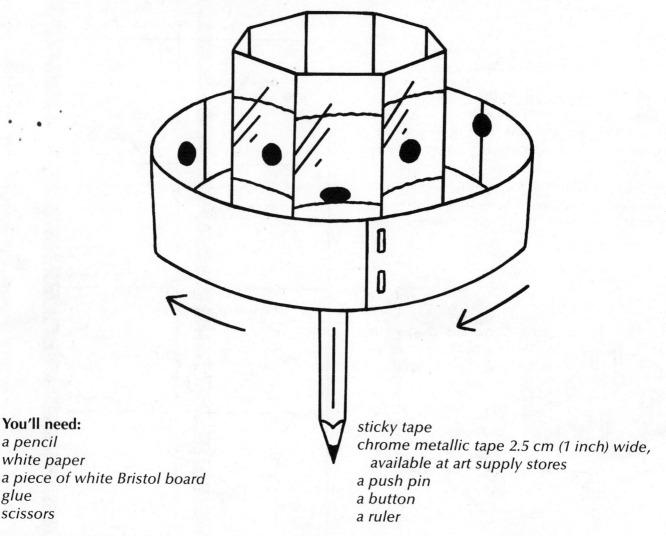

You'll need:
a pencil
white paper
a piece of white Bristol board
glue
scissors

sticky tape
chrome metallic tape 2.5 cm (1 inch) wide,
    available at art supply stores
a push pin
a button
a ruler

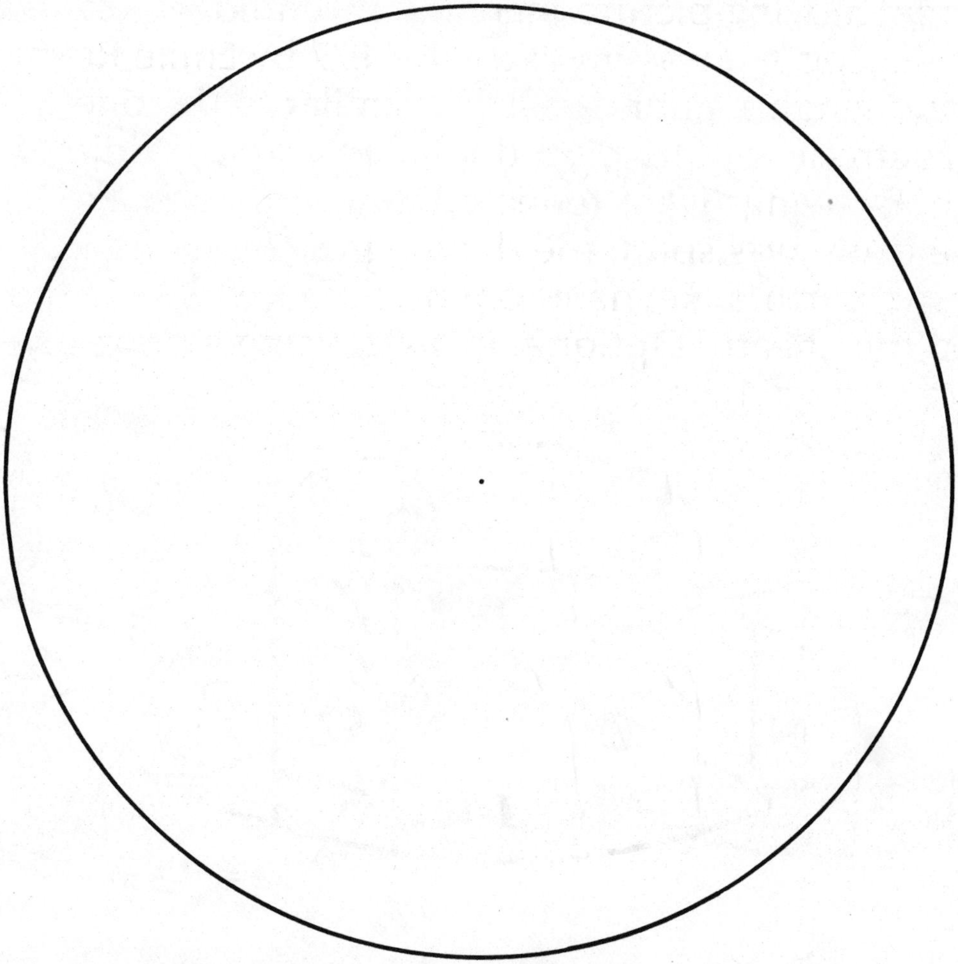

1 Cut out a strip of white Bristol board that is 3 cm (1¼ inches) wide and 42 cm (16½ inches) long. Bend this strip so that it forms a circle. Overlap the two end pieces so that 2 cm (¾ inch) on each end overlaps. Staple these two ends together.

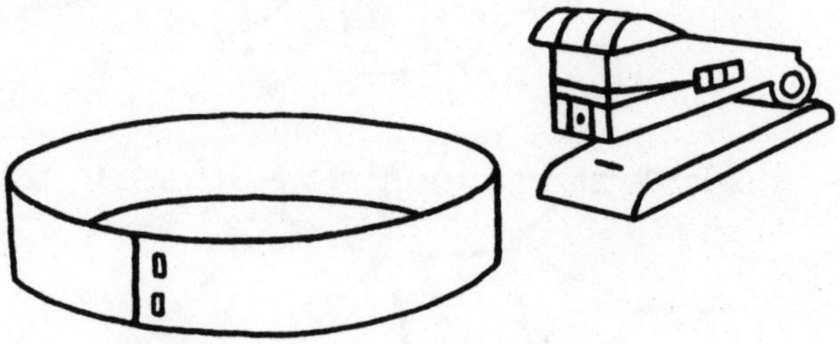

2 Trace the circle on this page onto a piece of white paper.

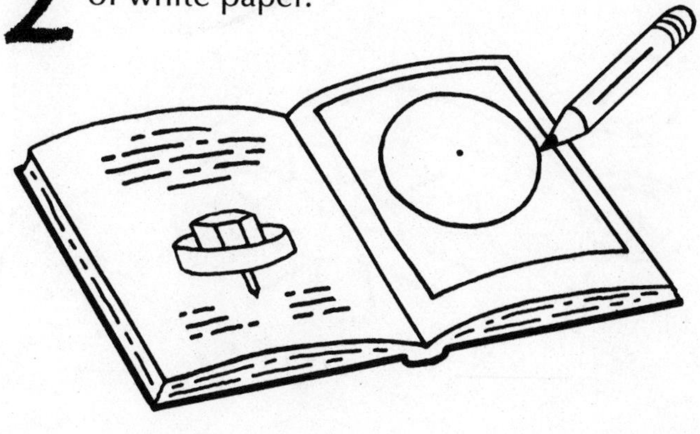

3 Glue the paper to a piece of white Bristol board.

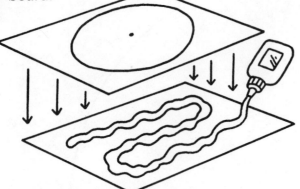

4 Cut out the Bristol board circle with your scissors.

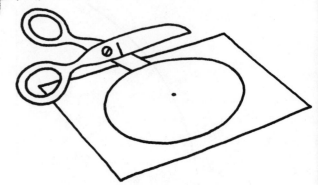

5 Tape the Bristol board circle to the strip you made in step 1.

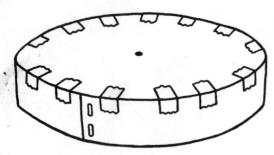

6 Trace the wheel figure on page 93 onto a piece of white paper, and glue the paper to a piece of white Bristol board as you did in step 3.

7 Cut out the wheel figure with your scissors.

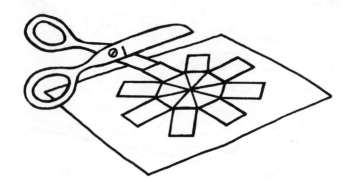

8 On the cardboard side of your wheel, tape a piece of chrome metallic tape to each panel as shown.

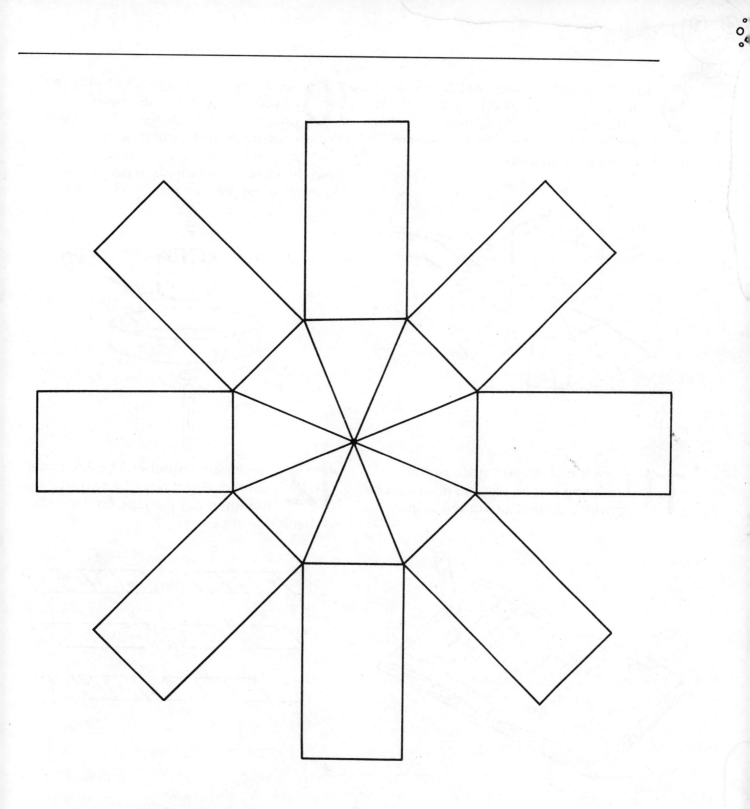

9 Turn the wheel back over to the paper side. Bend the panels up and tape them together on the inside as shown, so that you have a cylinder shape. The metallic tape should now be on the outside.

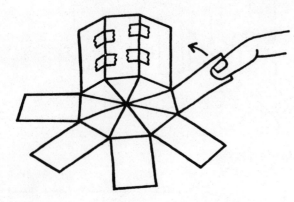

10 Tape this metallic cylinder to the middle of your bigger circle as shown. Use a push pin to line up the two centre holes. Place a button over the point of the pin and push the pin into the eraser end of a pencil. Spin the outside cylinder. If it doesn't spin easily, pull the pin out a bit.

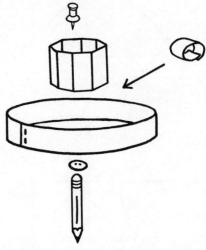

11 Trace the animation strips of the bouncing ball on page 95 onto a piece of white paper. Cut out the strips.

12 Place panel number 4 beside panel number 5 and tape the two strips together. Put the tape on the back so that it doesn't show.

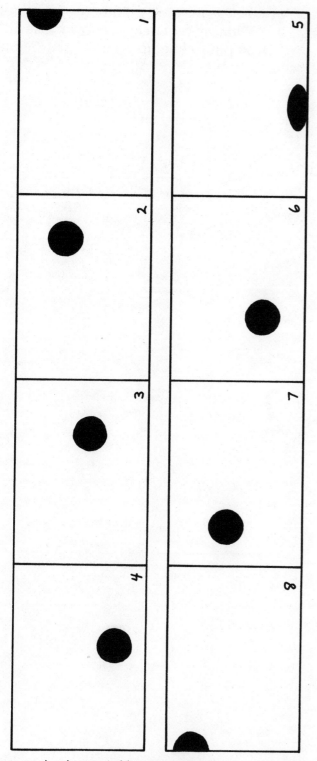

13 Place the animation strip inside the praxinoscope cylinder.

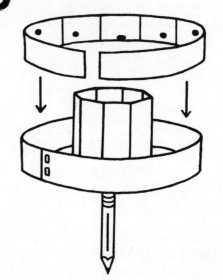

14 When you spin the outside cylinder and look into the metallic mirrors, you'll see the ball bouncing. Hold the praxinoscope under a light to make the animation show up better.

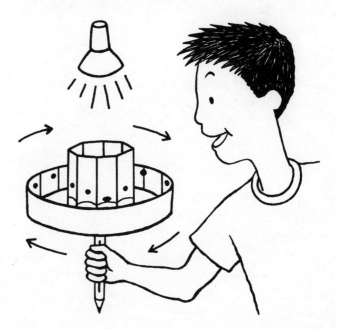